Planet Boomer

Planet Boomer

Retire now for less in
Southeast Asia

Jim Herrler • Ellen Ma

BARLOW

Library and Archives Canada Cataloguing in Publication data available upon request.

ISBN 978-0-9937656-8-1 (print)
ISBN 978-0-9937656-9-8 (ebook)

Printed in Canada

TO ORDER:
In Canada:
    Jaguar Book Group
    100 Armstrong Avenue, Georgetown, ON L7G 5S4

In the U.S.A.:
    Midpoint Book Sales & Distribution
    27 West 20th Street, Suite 1102, New York, NY 10011

SALES REPRESENTATION:
    Canadian Manda Group
    165 Dufferin Street, Toronto, ON M6K 3H6

Cover and interior design: Kyle Gell Design
Page layout: Kyle Gell Design
Production/Editorial: At Large Editorial Services
Cover images: (front cover) © Yangchao | Dreamstime.com,
    (back cover) © Rene Drouyer | Dreamstime.com

For more information, visit **www.barlowbooks.com**

Barlow Book Publishing Inc.
    96 Elm Avenue, Toronto, ON, Canada M4W 1P2

BARLOW

To my life and work partner, Ellen Ma.
Relentlessly objective, fiercely focused, and
dedicated to the destruction of all sacred cows.
There would be no book without you.

And to our partners and friends Stephen Wyatt
and Colleen Ryan. This was your idea. I just hope
we didn't screw it up. Thank you for your
guidance, your patience, and for all the
white wine in Byron Bay.

contents

Your Passport to Real Retirement Freedom

Freedom. It's about time.

There are not many periods in your life when you get to experience real freedom. Most of us enjoyed just that in our late teens and twenties, pre-marriage and before any kids arrived. Before mortgage and debt and work took on a great seriousness.

But once the kids are grown, debts are paid, and your working life is winding down, suddenly you enter another period of freedom.

Will you enjoy it now just as you did when you were twenty-one?

You can. All you need to do is to be clever and brave enough to change your lifestyle and leverage the benefits of that freedom.

It doesn't matter if you are 45 or nearly 65. If you have reached a turning point in your life, then clean the slate and look at all the options. Be brave.

And if you are facing retirement, then see it as an opportunity, not a death sentence. It is an extraordinary, once-in-a-lifetime opportunity to live your life to the fullest.

Isn't 60 supposed to be the new 40?

There are a few key decision-making moments in your life. One was back in the days when you chose a career; others were choosing whom to marry, where to live, whether to have children.

Now is the time to decide how to live your next life chapter. Do you stay put, age in place, and let the years pile on or do you reach for something more, something more inspiring? Whether you are burned out at 40 or facing the same old landscape at 60, making a bold change can be a fresh start on the rest of your life.

> *Once the kids are grown and become*
> *self-sufficient and once debts are paid and*
> *your working life ends, suddenly you enter*
> *another period of immense freedom—it's*
> *back to your 20s again.*

If you are one of Canada's 10 million baby boomers, chances are that the kids are grown (or nearly so), the dog is dead (or nearly so), your house is paid for (or nearly so), and the job is winding down or, in some cases, just too intolerable to put up with anymore.

But you have to soldier on. Ten more years, fifteen, twenty? That's what we do. It is our script.

The end game reads like this: stay in your home as long as you can, get another dog, hang about with the kids and grandkids, and learn to count your pennies because all those years of saving didn't get you as far as you thought. But that's okay, you'll spend your time at the same golf course, restaurants, clubs, and pubs you have always gone to. Watch more TV, trim those lawns to perfection, spend an extra two weeks at the cottage (but not too much; the bugs are bad in the spring and it gets cold in late October).

We can hear some of you saying that is exactly what you are looking forward to, what you've been working for. To many Canadians, thousands of you, however, it isn't enough. It is your parents' life and it doesn't have to be yours. Why raise the white flag when there is so much more living to do?

This book outlines an alternative in a Southeast Asian country. It offers a chance for a new life for six months, for a year, for a few years, or forever. And a less expensive life that will make your hard-earned dollars stretch further than they ever would at home.

It speaks to those who see impending retirement not as declining sunset years but as the dawn of an inspiring and exciting period of their lives. It speaks to Canadians of any age who defy the status quo—the expected outcome—and who relish the idea of living in a place where winter never comes. Even if it's just a temporary choice, from a few months to a longer term, you can extend your finances, sport a permanent tan, and get healthier as you run, swim, play tennis, or golf every day of the year.

Sure, you can do the "sensible" thing and decide not to indulge in a nice night out because you need to save up for that new snow blower or set aside extra money for the January gas bill.

Is that what's stopping you from your dream retirement?

Money? Maybe. But there is a bigger reason: *you*. You are the biggest obstacle between the retirement you can afford and the retirement you have dreamed about.

Intrigued? How about we get started.

part I

Sometimes We All Need a
Mindset Martini

chapter 1

Getting Started

et's face it, life has changed.

Many Canadians "found themselves" by travelling overseas when they were young. For a lot of them, that gap-year moment in time stuck to their psyche and never left. Recessive it may be but it is still there, an itch to be scratched that doesn't go away.

We can guess what you are thinking. It's probably something like "Sure, that's easy for them to say." If you want to know the truth, we thought the same thing. It was never our intention to retire overseas. It was absurd. And it wasn't an easy decision, but it was among the best decisions we ever made.

Relax that muscle you call your brain; let your imagination wander.

My first overseas adventure was going to Europe at 21. I have made hundreds of trips for business and pleasure all over the world since, but I didn't truly pack up and leave again until I was 55. In our travels over the last eight years in Asia, my wife and partner, Ellen, and I have met many hundreds of people of all ages and all nationalities. Some were here on just a two-year assignment but many more have begun the process of putting down roots here, buying condos or beachfront land because they are either coming back or never leaving. It's no longer a radical step for young professionals to live and work here, and it won't be any more radical for them to retire on a palm-fronted Thai beach in a gorgeous home, a home one-third the price of a Muskoka or Laurentian or Sunshine Coast property that gets used perhaps half the year.

Right, then. Sell your house. Tell the kids and grandkids you love them to death but that you're embarking on a wonderful adventure and so too are they.

You want them to be part of your new life, and this offers them their own share of your adventure, although not like every day you get to have. Take the housesale proceeds, bank them, call a taxi, go to the airport, get on a plane, get yourself a beach house in Malaysia, Bali, Thailand, Cambodia, or Vietnam. Let your new housekeeper manage the meals, pay the bills, and sweep the sand off the terrace. Go for a swim every morning. Watch the nightly news, or not. The family is coming over for Christmas and spring break and summer vacations—they will *love* it.

And guess what? It can all be done for a fraction of the cost of living at home in Canada. Sure, there are a few financial considerations and visa issues, but these are easily handled. If you are of the age when you are on a pension, in most instances our government will pay it into your local bank in your new country.

Perfect, eh?

RADICAL OR SABBATICAL?

Of course, taking off to Southeast Asia permanently is a radical approach to a pre-retirement or full-retirement life change. Any move overseas requires a lot more research, and that is what this book is all about.

Change can be modest or aggressive.

The fact is you can be very modest in your planning; rent your house at home versus selling it; go for the 183 days a year Canada allows you to leave the country and maintain all your benefits. You can still cut your costs dramatically.

The rental income from your house at home will cover both your airfare *and* rental costs in Southeast Asia.

Also, the move may be just for a few years or less—a kind of sabbatical or extended holiday from your life in Canada.

THE ESCAPE SPECTRUM

Not everyone is ready for the full monty. Some of us who feel the itch are not ready to commit. No problem. There is a spectrum of escape, from running away forever to leaving for just a few months at a time. To put it simply, your options are these:

1. Take off. Live in a wonderful new place that is cheaper, and do it for the long term.
2. Pack up. Keep the family home in Canada, rent it out, and go and live in a place you've always dreamed of.
3. Refresh and recharge. Take the full six months our government allows, or any amount of time it takes for your renewed happiness.

We think the beauty of this is that no matter who you are, how rich or poor you are, or how old you are there is an escape route that will suit you. The need to get away is often triggered by external factors—things like a financial crisis, an illness or death in the family, an inheritance, or the end of one's working life.

We all will need to adapt to some sort of life change eventually. Many people approaching retirement dropped a bundle in the global financial crisis when the stock market halved in 2008–2009. Can it happen again? Will housing prices continue to soar for the next decade? Will interest rates always be this low? The answers to these questions aren't always encouraging. If your nest egg has been crushed or if, in fact, you never had a big enough nest egg in the first place, then a long life in Canada can become cripplingly expensive. One solution is to move to a cheaper country and make those scarce funds stretch a lot further.

My wife and I did. We rented and then later sold our house, along with our skis, boots, and winter coats. We gave up our residency (and Canadian taxes), then got on a plane.

> Take the funds from the sale or rental of your
> house. Call a taxi. Go to the airport. Get on a plane.
> Go and live a life of comfort and pleasure. Get a
> house on the beach in Bali, Malaysia, Thailand,
> Vietnam, or Cambodia. It's doable. There are
> few financial constraints and any visa issues
> can be easily handled.

WHY US? WHY NOT YOU?

Eight years ago Ellen and I left corporate life in Toronto for a new life in Asia. At home we had big jobs, big salaries, big bonuses, sexy German cars, an enormous downtown renovated house, and a mountain of more or less manageable debt. Then it ended abruptly for both of us. Our fancy jobs disappeared.

After a year of testing the waters of independence, we realized that the corporate work life we had known wasn't going to happen for us again. At least not in as grand a fashion. Why? In part we didn't want it anymore, at least not enough to make the personal and professional sacrifices required. I recall vividly the moment years earlier when we bought our huge house and embarked upon the costly top-to-bottom renovation. My company's chairman said with a wry smile that he liked his employees to be "debt motivated."

We didn't want to fall into that trap again.

Upon winding up my role in Canada, my company's head office in New York sent me to Hong Kong to assist on a pitch for a global brand—and the Asia bug bit, and bit hard. On my return after six weeks, Ellen and I began plotting how and where we could get to in Asia. Fortunately, Ellen's corporate connections turned up a position in Singapore, and we were on our way. The house was rented out to a lovely New York couple, the garage sale and Goodwill drop-offs were completed, and we landed in Singapore in the late fall of 2006.

I had transferred an employee to my former company's Singapore office a year earlier, and it turned out to have been a fortunate move for us. She was and is one of the world's great connectors. With her help, in weeks we had a new gang of expat friends from all over the world, and we settled into a gorgeous rented condo on the Singapore River with a huge terrace from which you could step right into the pool. The first winter passed with long Sunday lunches inevitably ending up with a dozen people lounging in the sun or more splashing about in the pool. By then I was working on a project for a Saudi prince and made four trips to Riyadh in the first two years while Ellen toiled away in the tech business in a regional role. We made less money, but due to the incredibly low taxes in Singapore, we were keeping much more of it. Our new life was so good, you'd think we had actually planned it for years.

The weekends were our open window on Asia. We began frequenting Bali (at last count we have been fourteen times) followed by Bangkok, Phuket, and Krabi in Thailand; Hanoi in Vietnam; and Beijing and Shanghai just in our first year! Now, we have made over fifty trips to cities and resorts in North- and Southeast Asia plus Australia, New Zealand, India, and Sri Lanka.

After two years in Singapore, an exciting opportunity took us to Shanghai, where we had an even more dynamic experience that included the Beijing Olympics in 2008 and the Shanghai Expo a year later. Due to the transient nature of Asian business postings, many of our Singapore friends wound up in Shanghai, with many more going back and forth on a regular basis.

We took one trip home to Canada a year, every year, to see family and friends. It was enough for us to remain connected and look after our rented house until we sold it to our tenants in our fourth year away.

We never went home in winter and haven't seen snow or experienced cold in over eight years. Well, I did see snow on a distant mountain in New Zealand, and we had one snow flurry in Shanghai one evening, but that was it. We replaced the cold white stuff with the warm white sand of dozens of idyllic beaches.

After three fascinating years in Shanghai, we returned to Singapore to open our own company and quickly fell right back into the life we had before.

But it wasn't quite the same. Under the banner of "you can never go back," Singapore had become frightfully expensive in the three years we had been away. Living in one of the few real nanny states where your every move is under the eyes of an all-seeing one-party government, we started to feel more nervous than we should have been at visa renewal time. The process of writing this book had begun, and as we travelled about Southeast Asia, we realized there was another kind of life to be had. One where the cost of living is a fraction of what it is at home in Canada (and in Singapore), where the health care is excellent, where you could live a *very* comfortable life among charming people while stretching your scarce resources far beyond what you ever thought was possible.

This revelation was not just a random or nice-to-know observation. We needed it ourselves. The 2008–2009 financial crisis battered our investments and lost us years of growth. For the last eight key earning years since we left the well-paid corporate world, our nomadic lifestyle has left us short of our goals. Of course, we need to make more money, but we also need to stretch what we have.

TO LIVE WELL FOR LESS

Recently, we made another move and later in the book, once you've read all the choices we have uncovered, we will tell you why we chose this place and what our new life is like.

The point of this intro is to show that we did it and you can do it too. This book is a no-holds-barred guide to what we think are the five most appealing countries in Southeast Asia and fifteen destinations where you can live a better full- or part-time retirement life than you can at home in Canada.

Some destinations are fully developed and ready for you today. Others are developing and a work-in-progress that may (or may not) become preferred landing spots a few years from now. All are exotic in their own ways and all are worthy of consideration depending on the level of comfort or adventure you seek.

In our travels for this book, we have met and interviewed dozens of people with stories of their own to tell. Some wanted off the work treadmill, some realized that a comfortable retirement at home was way out of reach, and some wanted more adventure in their lives. All refused to age in place and accept the cards dealt to them. They wanted a new deal.

Don't you?

THE CHECKLIST

Not so fast.

This type of change isn't for everybody. Some of our closest friends have never come close to visiting us in the eight-plus years we've been away while people we knew much less well have come to see us many times. While we remain on the Canadian radar, our home away is too far or just not of sufficient interest to some compared to their familiar turf. That's okay. We get it. Not for everyone.

We hope that you read further and discover what really is possible. But keeping in mind the above, here is a cheeky checklist to help determine if this part of the world is a possibility for you.

It goes like this:

1. I have more than enough money to retire. I like five months of snow and ice. Too much sun gives me a rash. Put the book down.

2. My children need me and will until they are 30 or older. I
   can't leave them alone without my ongoing support ($$$).
   Put the book down.
3. Do they have Harvey's Bacon Cheeseburgers, Swiss Chalet
   Half Chicken Dinners, Triple O's, or Tim's Double Doubles?
   Put the book down.
4. I love my house, I love my car, I love my cottage, I love
   my golf club, I love paying Canadian taxes, I love Cana-
   dian politics, especially Rob Ford and his whole family.
   They will rise again.
   Put the book down.
5. It's too far. Flights cost too much. I get violently airsick
   after three hours.
   Put the book down.

Seriously, this book isn't for people with pots of money. They have the means to make their own choices. It is for the people who don't have enough to live the life they would like to have.

You may be surprised to find your kids will visit frequently and Skype or FaceTime keeps you up to date between visits. We Skype almost daily, and in our business we electronically transfer funds all over the world.

Missing comfort food? Southeast Asia may well have the tastiest and healthiest food in the world. Every country of the five we cover has unique and truly wonderful fare for no more than the change in your pocket.

And if the things listed above are stuff you must have, that you truly love, then a move like this is probably not right for you.

Finally, there is no denying it is a long way to fly—twelve hours at a minimum. But really, that is dinner, a good movie, an episode of *Modern Family*, an Ambien, and breakfast. As to cost, there are options galore beyond the outrageous pricing and limited destinations of our national airline. In 2014, we flew premium economy on Cathay Pacific from Bangkok to New York return for $1,750 each. Personally, I think the premium is worth it, but fly economy if you must for $1,000 each.

You can do this. Explore the book's stories to find out how others did it and determine if their experiences reflect the realities that you face. You will find remarkable similarities regardless of where people come from: Canada, England, Australia, America, et cetera.

Most of us went to work in our early 20s. We saw our parents' wealth grow as they aged and, to a large degree, realized that it grew because they played the real estate market very well. They had pensions at work and drove Pontiacs, maybe a Buick if they were flush. Life was pretty good for them, and most of us thought we could do even better.

Our reality is different today. There are few company pensions left if you don't have a government job. Unions have largely been rendered toothless by global companies that would rather close or relocate than bend to labour demands. Manufacturing went offshore and banking went from the un-sexiest job ever to the coolest way to make money without really making anything. Our RRSP growth was pretty good until the downturn of 2008 and 2009; by now we might have clawed back most or all of it, though, even if we missed out on five or six key growth years.

We soldiered on, building equity in our homes, having kids, summering at a Canadian lake, and then the hammer fell for many people.

The math wasn't working anymore.

Something went wrong, and as we looked down the road, it got worse.

You may have felt it at 50, or 55, or 60-plus. Life just kicked you in the ass—it's a wake-up call you need to answer.

chapter 2

Can You Afford To?
You Can't Afford *Not* To!

T he idea of moving to a less expensive country is increasingly appealing to baby boomers. For many it will become a necessity, and you are not going to be alone.

Governments, analysts, and economists in the developed Western world are increasingly frightened that we will be unable to look after our aging population. If they know it, South and Central American countries know it and Southeast Asian countries know it too. They have been busy preparing for your arrival.

There is a new diaspora—an international shift of people over 50 moving from the developed world to the more affordable developing world where they can afford a better life in retirement.

WHY AND WHY *NOW?*

The Canadian Census of 2011 showed 9.6 million people are aged 44 to 64—the baby boomers. In twenty-five years, the number of us who are 65 or over will double.

And we are living longer.

It's the same story in the United States and other developed countries. Over the next forty years, the number of people in the United States over 60 is expected to double to a staggering number, over 80 million people.

The implications of these demographic shifts are becoming glaringly obvious. The cost of caring for this increased longevity will soar. And since the West has done little to realign its medical infrastructure from critical care to the very different needs of an aging population, there will not be enough resources to go around. Services will be stretched beyond all limits and the tab for this will land, as it usually does, on all of us in the forms of huge tax loads to bandage failed systems. In just the next few years, six out of ten Canadian provinces will be spending more than 50 per cent of their revenues on health care. Ontario and Quebec have already hit that number. Health care costs are increasing and could well become unsustainable—Canada does not have a history of government managing this kind of change well.

The other, and even scarier, consequence of this aging boomer cohort is a financial one—they have not put aside enough money for retirement.

A CIBC poll conducted in 2011 found only half of Canadians aged 44 to 64 have a regular retirement savings program in place. Not to put too much faith in our banks' self-serving research, but a poll by BMO the same year indicated that the nearly 10 million Canadian baby boomers are on average $400,000 *short of their ideal retirement goal.*

Did they also know they would likely be living ten years longer than their parents?

In 2011 Canada had 9.6 million baby boomers 44 to 64 years of age. By 2036, the number of people 65 and over will have doubled.

Western governments cannot make up the difference. It's questionable if they can even keep current payments and programs in place let alone account for inflation. In Canada, we are better off than most countries, having revamped our social security to keep existing programs viable for the next few years, but that is just the existing programs, not dramatically expanded ones.

Governments in Southeast Asia see this looming retirement income gap as an opportunity to utilize their lower costs to trigger investment in relevant retirement services to satisfy these needs.

There is a new diaspora—a community of people over 50 moving from the developed world to the much less expensive developing countries. To varying degrees, these countries are ready. Their advantage was starting from scratch. No legacy issues, no sacred cows. Some started years ago, some are just beginning to put programs in place.

We've investigated five Southeast Asian countries: Indonesia (Bali), Thailand, Malaysia, Vietnam, and Cambodia. Some countries already have excellent infrastructure in place for expats. Others are a work-in-progress that may (or may not) evolve into a fully serviced destination for full- or part-time retirees in a few years. The ones we haven't covered here are, in our opinion, not ready and most likely aren't going to be any time soon.

Singapore has become *way* too expensive (we know, we lived there) and the Philippines lacks security and good infrastructure, as does Laos. Sri Lanka has been a political minefield since its civil war ended in 2009, and a new government may, or may not, effect real change; Myanmar is far too rough around the edges and has only recently become a decent tourist destination. All are fabulous for a visit but that's about it right now.

Our three years in China were an unforgettable adventure. We loved the experience, but the high cost, congestion, pollution, and politics keep both Mainland China and Hong Kong off our retirement list.

THE BOOK AND HOW TO USE IT

This book is a tool, a guide for people to initiate a process of consideration. In it you will find interviews with people like you who have done it, who made the move to a Southeast Asian country. Their reasons may differ; some were economic, some were personal. We met a lot of people who just wanted to enjoy a rich and luxurious retirement but on a budget they could afford—and they found it. Others we met were seeking a more adventurous life. They found it, too. And so can you.

In each country chapter, we touch on the place itself to give the reader some context. We realize when you think of the ideal retirement location, places like Italy or France leap to mind; we get it. We thought so too. But think about it: everyone else in the world is thinking the same thing. And that is the big reason why it's mind-bogglingly expensive in key areas and heavily taxed as well.

What we are asking you to consider is this: your dream retirement location is out there—you just might need a bigger list. So these thumbnail intros are designed to break the ice, to get you to warm up to a new idea. However, this is not a travel book, and while we introduce a bit of history, politics, and economics to give you context, there are many resource books and websites to give you the deeper details this book does not include.

We are not shy. If, in our judgment, we believe there is an issue that needs to be identified, we spare no sacred cows in bringing it up. Thus our opinions may not suit all readers and certainly not all governments. So be it.

In every country chapter and for every destination, we try to provide a real-time day-to-day flavour of expat life from people who are already living it. We use accepted, quantifiable cost-of-living comparisons, the most recent available. For consistency, all local currencies shown have been converted to Canadian dollars at rates current at the time of this writing. The visa and immigration information is highlighted in the country chapters with much more detail in the support chapters. However, government policies do change (both for the short term and long term) and we encourage you to seek up-to-date information as even the most sophisticated countries are making adjustments to their rules and requirements on a regular basis. This is particularly true in the property sections, where we discuss buying versus renting. (Just so you know, in almost every circumstance we suggest renting to start, as in "look before you leap." But more on that later.)

Getting comfortable in a new country takes a little time and adjustment; some warm to their adopted country quickly, some take a little time, some never do. In our case, moving to Singapore nearly ten years ago wasn't much of a shock. It was and is a *very* sophisticated, modern city that offers every comfort and convenience you have at home. In fact, it has better transit, better Wi-Fi, the best airport in the world, and much lower taxes at a maximum of 17 per cent before deductions. Now, however, the cost of living has become terribly expensive. And it appears to be by design. The government wants Singapore to be the Monaco of Asia. That leaves room for other countries to create environments just as appealing but a whole lot cheaper.

Each chapter has a quick summary called Tips and Traps, little things we learned from our own experiences. At the end of each country chapter, we have our "thumbs up or thumbs down" checklist. Here, we summarize the country against five key criteria: cost of living, health care, buying or renting property, visas, and immigration.

Finally, go to our website www.planet-boomer.com. Get to meet the people in the book, and see pictures of where they live. Read our visitor forums and look for updates from our partner interviewees on their experiences.

RETIRE IN ASIA? *REALLY?* REALLY!

Yes, really. It is a viable option for people who want a different kind of retirement and, more importantly, for people who just can't afford to retire at home.

There is a residual impression in the West—we have heard it even among people we know well—that this part of Asia is still third world, a place where natives live in huts, dine on strange creatures, and get their health care from the local medicine man. That is an exaggeration, of course, but in the remotest areas of many of the countries we cover in the book, you will discover people who do live very simple lives. For us and for many of our expat friends, that is a plus.

The reality of Southeast Asia is that for every good there is a little bad. Then again, a lot of it has to do with what you think is good or bad. And that is what makes Southeast Asia so rich and exotic: it is not two-dimensional.

Much of Southeast Asia is for the most part indistinguishable from any modern city or region in Europe or North America. There are gorgeous condominiums, villas, and homes that span a wide variety of locations on the beach, in the cities, or on the mountainsides. These places can cost as little as hundreds of dollars a month to rent and, in many cases, less than $100,000 to buy. Set a target for your maximum outlay. A rule of thumb we've found useful is to aim at a 50 per cent reduction in overall costs as a starting point. And you can do better than that.

Sound tempting? It should. But that is just to start.

The food in Southeast Asia is among the freshest, healthiest, and *best in the world*. From Vietnam to Malaysia, you will never lack for fantastic local food and great Western fare, if that is to your taste. Street food (or hawker stand food as we call it here) is always fresh and always prepared right in front of you. You can't say that about a Big Mac, but that too is available throughout Asia.

We have found, country by country, that you can have a great meal and a beer, eating locally, for as little as $5. Think about that: a complete delicious meal plus a beer for about what you would pay for a large coffee and doughnut at Tim's. And if you wish white-tablecloth service, it's available and it's fantastic—and it will easily be 50 to 60 per cent cheaper than in Toronto or Calgary or Vancouver.

Again, we are not expecting you to settle for less. What we are asking you to consider is the idea of getting *a lot more* than you ever dreamed of and all of it for a hell of a lot less than you could ever imagine.

With regard to health care, we have come to realize that the impression that "West is best" under all circumstances just isn't always true anymore. As our baby boomer demographic grows at home, it will be access to care that gets increasingly difficult. How long does it take now to get seen in Emergency? To get an MRI or a CAT scan? Even necessary surgeries can be delayed for weeks or perhaps months.

Now consider what happens as the baby boomer cohort numbers over 65 start to creep up, eventually more than doubling the current size?

Do you really think Canadian medical services will get better? That our access to high-quality care will magically be delivered more efficiently and when we need it rather than when they can fit us in? And can our current critical care focus adapt to the different care needs of an aging population?

In many parts of Southeast Asia, this isn't an issue. Our own experience is that you can get an MRI on the day you request it, have it read by a trained professional, and embark on a course of treatment, should you need it, *immediately*. Hospitals are state of the art in Singapore, Bangkok, Chiang Mai, Kuala Lumpur, and Penang, and there are often half a dozen or more facilities per market, regardless of the size of the local population.

This is the result of medical tourism, a system where medical services cater to the needs of offshore patients at reasonable prices in five-star facilities. We have learned of many expat retirees in Southeast Asia who have opted to forgo health insurance completely. As the costs of coverage have risen steadily or they discover that they cannot qualify for coverage because of pre-existing conditions, they find it makes more sense to use the money they were paying for that increasingly expensive insurance to top up an emergency bank balance on a regular basis. That money is meant to cover major issues, and anything else can be easily paid out-of-pocket. Something more to consider:

it isn't simply a question of access. Attitude is important. We have found—and our expat friends agree—that throughout Southeast Asia there is a deep and prevalent cultural legacy of respect for older people. Overall, the level of caregiving for them is unrivalled and the cost is remarkably affordable. It is a health care recipe we think works on all counts.

Our eight-plus years of experience in the region and our dozens of interviews with expat retirees over five countries in fourteen destinations is proof positive this is a solution for many Canadians facing a less-than-comfortable future at home.

TIPS AND TRAPS

As you read this book and consider the possibilities of a life in Southeast Asia, remember that the secret to every good trip is in the planning.

We include plenty of details throughout the book to help plan your overseas adventure, but to get you started here is a quick checklist of questions you must address before you put the snow shovel away for good and pack up the flannel shirts for charity.

Visas: How do I choose the right visa for my needs once I decide on the country I would like to live in?

Taxation: Am I better off as a non-resident of Canada to avoid taxes? Should I instead maintain all my benefits by going offshore only part-time?

RRSP: What happens to my RRSP if I leave the country? Can I still contribute? Can I withdraw without penalty?

My house: If I rent my house, am I taxed on the rental income? If I sell, how does capital gains tax apply?

Pension: If I am of retirement age, can my pension(s) be paid in my new country?

Health insurance: If I leave the country full-time, will I need health insurance and what kind? If it is just part-time, is my Canadian coverage sufficient overseas?

These are just some of the hard questions we answer, as well as address the real costs of living that will make such a difference to your finances. We also, through interviews and personal experiences, answer the soft questions. Soft they may be, but they are critical to having a happy and fulfilling life overseas. Is English spoken there? Is there a community to engage with? Will I be safe? How accessible is the internet and can I get my Apple computer fixed? The answer to all these questions is yes; everything you can do at home, you can do here. Often even better. And if a fear of all these strange languages makes you hesitant, take a lesson from me. My language skills never got any better than high school French. But in every country I've been in, either English is common or you get by beautifully with a smile and a greeting in the local language. Hey, if I can learn that much, so can you.

Let's go and find out.

Southeast Asia

CHINA

INDIA

TAIWAN

PHILIPPINES

Manila ★

PALAU

Melekeok ★

FEDERATED STATES
OF MICRONESIA

PAPUA
NEW GUINEA

Hagåtña

MYANMAR
(BURMA)

Yangon ★
(Rangoon)

THAILAND

Bangkok ★

LAOS

Vientiane ★

VIETNAM

Hanoi ★

CAMBODIA

Phnom
Penh ★

Gulf of
Tonkin

MALAYSIA

Kuala
Lumpur ★

SINGAPORE

BRUNEI

Bandar Seri Begawan ★

INDONESIA

Jakarta ★

TIMOR LESTE

AUSTRALIA

BANGLADESH

BHUTAN

Thimphu ★

Kathmandu ★

SRI
LANKA

Colombo ★

MALDIVES

Male ★

Philippine Sea

South China
Sea

Celebes Sea

Luzon
Strait

Gulf of
Thailand

Andaman
Sea

Bay of
Bengal

Laccadive
Sea

INDIAN OCEAN

Arafura Sea

Timor Sea

Gulf of
Carpentaria

part II

Welcome to Your
New Life!

chapter 3

Bali:
The Island of the Gods

Bali has held a magical mystique on expats for over one hundred years.

Think of a sun-kissed island with frangipani-scented evenings and incense-rich temple sunrises off white-sand beaches. It's an image that has captivated Western travellers for more than one hundred years. In more recent times, millions were enchanted by the depiction of Bali from the best-selling book and hit movie *Eat, Pray, Love* and imagined themselves as Julia Roberts or Javier Bardem being swept away by Bali's intoxicating charms. Well, some did.

No surprise then that it is the first of our retirement destinations to explore. Can the spirituality and charm of the movie myth match the reality?

GETTING TO KNOW BALI

With 238 million people spread over 17,508 islands (I know, I counted!), Indonesia has the fourth-largest population in the world. The republic in total is 87 per cent Muslim with a small 3 per cent Hindu minority. Over the centuries, Indonesia, and particularly Java (the most populous island), became increasingly Muslim dominated; Bali became the default Hindu home base and now, with a population that is 85 per cent Hindu, it is by far the dominant religion on the island.

Why does that matter? It would be unfair to simply describe a Hindu majority as an easier group for expats to cohabit with, but there is some truth to that. In matters from social interaction to real estate, the Balinese Hindu majority is more amenable, less strict in religious beliefs, and more comfortable with foreigners than Muslims are. And though there are many other beautiful islands in Indonesia, only Bali can offer the infrastructure a Westerner tends to require. Bali checks all those boxes. Here you will find good cellular networks and wireless, Western supermarkets, alcohol (that's a big one), a booming real estate market, English widely spoken, and an expat community of over 10,000 including 2,500 retirees.

Bali is only 8 degrees south of the equator. For all of you who aren't geography majors, that's 600 miles (965 kilometres). The weather is tropical year round; temperatures average about 86 degrees Fahrenheit (30 degrees Celsius) with two distinct seasons. The *wet* is December through March; the *dry* is April through November. Even in the wet season the sun can burst out a minute after a downpour. Humidity ranges from a pleasant 65 per cent in the dry season (about the same as Hawaii) to a sticky 85 per cent in the wet months. Yeah, that's unpleasant. But here is how I learned to deal with it: slow down, sit in the shade, relax, and have a beer or two. And just keep thinking, this sure beats Winnipeg in January. Or February. Or March, April ... well, you get the idea. The proximity to the equator moderates extremes so there are no typhoons, tornadoes, or cyclones.

Sound good?

On paper and at first glance, Bali looks perfect. Although on the surface it can be, there are some important caveats. Serious efforts must be made for it to realize its potential as a long-term destination for Canadian retirees. It is a stunningly beautiful, wine-glass–shaped island with most of its 4.2 million people concentrated in the south. Nearer the middle is the ancient cultural hub of Ubud (again, see *Eat, Pray, Love*—and relax, that's the last time we'll mention it) and most everything north of that is verdant jungle and mountains dominated by Mount Agung, an active volcano that last erupted in 1963.

The 3.2 million foreign tourists are found largely in southern towns like Kuta, Seminyak, Jimbaran, Nusa Dua, and Sanur. The capital, Denpasar, is almost a dividing line between "old" developed Bali (think tourism in areas like Kuta or Seminyak) and the "new" Bali with its very modern five-star hotels and million-dollar villas of the south shore and the underdeveloped more rugged north. Bali is also a popular destination for Indonesians from Jakarta. Many have holiday homes and/or keep cars and motorcycles there out of the eyes of the big-city taxman.

Since the infamous Bali bombings by off-island Islamic terrorists in 2002 and 2005, years of increased security have brought back a sense of calm and order to what has always been the most peaceful of all the islands. Tourism has returned in a big way and currently exceeds pre-bombing numbers with over 3 million visitors a year and still growing. Bali's permanent population has spiked as well, having experienced its largest growth rates in history. This is paradise at a price.

While tourism jobs fuel the local economy, the surge has led to rampant development that has severely taxed the limited infrastructure of Bali. Nearly unrestricted building of villas, hotels, and retail continues, and Bali's once abundant natural resources are increasingly stretched. Consider these numbers. Bali Tourism now states there are 100,000 hotel rooms on the island. The projected need to accommodate 3 million tourists was 38,000 rooms. Even if foreign tourist arrivals double (as projected) to 6 million or more by 2019, there are still too many rooms and more are being built every day. Add to that the over 7 million Indonesians who holiday in Bali every year, and then double that number too, and you have 20 million tourists by 2019 and no corresponding infrastructure being built (power, water, waste management) to support it. It is no wonder that current hotel occupancies of starred hotels hover around 53 per cent—a rule of thumb for break-even is 70 per cent. This is not a plan; it is unrestrained, out-of-the-park growth that defies all current laws, including a 2011 moratorium on building more hotel rooms that everyone simply ignored.

Bali now generates 26,160 cubic yards (20,000 cubic metres) of garbage a day, 1.3 cubic yards (1 cubic metre) for each of its 20,000 temples and shrines. Seventy-five per cent of the garbage goes uncollected. Bali's water table has been drained by unrestrained development: hotels, villas, golf courses, and hundreds of illegal wells have led to island-wide water shortages. The island's power supply is barely adequate and brownouts can be frequent. One might ask if these problems are not solvable with decent planning and investment. The answer is yes. Except ...

Indonesia's infamous but, sadly, well-deserved reputation for corruption historically has diverted public funding targeted to critical infrastructure improvements to, well, let's just say less deserving areas. Meanwhile, all those swanky new tourist villas, hotels, and golf courses just keep being built: some with permits, some without. It can't go on forever before it hits a critical point.

But we think positive change can save Bali.

Despite all the underlying problems, Bali is still one of the most beautiful places on earth. If the government, investors, hoteliers, and the Balinese people can get a grip on managing this growth, Bali is well worth considering for our generation and the next.

Bali still has the magic to intoxicate and enchant—as any expat there will admit.

Geoffrey and Michael

Geoffrey and Michael live upcountry in Ubud, in the spiritual heartland of Bali. It is the centre of the island, just 14 miles (24 kilometres) from the coast. Both of them spent most of their careers involved in the arts. Geoffrey ran a hotel with an entertainment theme and at one time was head of cultural affairs for Sydney, Australia, during the 2000 Olympics as well as CEO of the Australian Film Institute. Michael was an executive chef and went from entertaining customers to produce three musicals for the Sydney Opera House. When their working lives started to wind down, they crunched the numbers on their finances and realized they had to do something dramatic or face a very ordinary future in retirement.

"We were on two good salaries, living in a fabulous apartment and having a wonderful time," Michael said. "We had always been renters and had no equity in a house, so the prospect of retiring on reduced income meant our lifestyle would change in a major way."

The prospect of an underfunded retirement forced them to look at alternatives. "I recall we calculated that, on our pensions, the only alternative for us would have been to live in a trailer park in a second-tier town. So we really had to find somewhere we could live a reasonable, affordable life ... and Bali became a possibility," Geoffrey said.

"We had only been to Bali once before we moved here," he added. "We went to visit an old friend of ours. As a traveller, I had avoided the place as the stories of Kuta Beach as a spring-break-type hangout didn't appeal to us."

That was a decade ago. On their first visit, they found their friend lived in a beautiful old French villa in Ubud overlooking the Ayang River, where many five-star hotels like the Amandari and the Four Seasons are now located. They were inspired. "We planned to explore all of Bali but we never left Ubud. The first two weeks were spent on daybeds just admiring the stunning vista of the river below and nine-hundred-year-old rice paddies on its banks," said Michael.

Ubud nestles in the foothills of Bali's central mountain range. It is the cultural hub of the island, and the town is dotted with exquisite temples and ancient palaces alongside rich tropical gardens and rainforest.

"We saw that a good life here was possible," said Michael. "We've always been adventurers and always dreamt of going to live in Italy or Spain and learning a new language. Now, we thought, we can do it right here." Geoffrey and Michael noted that the Ubud Writers & Readers Festival has now been going on for more than ten years, and that was a key part of their decision to move there. "That a village like this in a foreign country is running a top English-language international writers festival really showed us there would be conversation here, an intellectual life here and ... people to talk to," said Geoffrey.

And among a community of expats, it is a fresh start with another language and a new culture, something to learn, to stay engaged. It was the adventure they wanted, that they could never afford to have retiring at home.

The defining moment for them was finding a piece of land on a quiet lane close by Ubud's charming town centre. For $65,000 (remember, these are Canadian-dollar equivalents) they leased it for twenty years with an additional ten-year option and built a traditional open-plan house with lush gardens, a stunning pool, and a guest house snuggled into a garden corner.

That was in 2010. Prices have risen since then but such a build can still be done and at a fraction of the price of just about anywhere in Canada—most especially in large metropolitan areas such as Toronto, Vancouver, Montreal, or Calgary.

Thanks to Bali, their financial worries are now behind them. They can live comfortably on their combined pensions of about $30,000 a year, in a lovely house with a full-time maid and two part-time helpers.

They are not alone.

For $65,000 all in, they bought a twenty-year lease with a ten-year option on the land and built a classic Javanese "joglo," an open-plan house, leading to lush gardens and a beautiful pool.

Paul and Kate

Bali is a leading-edge destination of a mini-wave of migration to Southeast Asia. But it isn't just retirees—the island appeals to people of all ages. There is a vibrant foreign community here as the island provides the kinds of services expats look for. And by that, I don't mean basic needs fulfilled (unless a basic need for you is a Double Double). Paul and Kate found much more.

The two of them, who are around 50, moved to Bali simply because they could live both cheaply and better than at home. Paul is an IT professional who works remotely, and Kate is a stay-at-home mum. They became members of the Canggu Club, just inland of the Canggu Beach area a mile or so up the coast from busy Seminyak.

The Canggu Club is a sprawling, white-washed, colonial complex overlooking immaculate playing fields. Undercover tennis courts are off to the left, enabling year-round play through the wet season. A large pool sits alongside the clubhouse. Sun lounge chairs, adorned with perfectly rolled blue-and-red-striped towels, surround the pool. Large teak French doors, with crisply painted white frames, lead to the club's indoor facilities, which include restaurants, a huge gym, a library, internet room, and kids' play area. There are squash courts and a bowling alley, and the Australian owners have just completed building a giant water park for kids.

The place is pristine and the membership is 100 per cent made up of expats, who pay an all-in annual adult membership of $1,300 per individual or a simple day pass for $22. Your maid gets in free.

The club is a haven for yummy mummies taking yoga classes while their kids take tennis lessons. The staff is predominantly Balinese and the members are certainly not—Australians and Brits dominate. At one point during our conversation in the club's café, Paul suddenly said, "That's him—that's the porn star." You probably don't hear that at the Boulevard Club in Toronto or the Arbutus Club in Vancouver, but it seems to fit here. A club with a porn star. Perhaps this is what colonial life has become, present day.

But living in Bali is not all about the Canggu Club or even its Western comforts and clubby scenarios (including the porn star). While it may suit some people looking for familiar themes, the island of Bali provides a real alternative to your life at home. It's about finding a new, exciting, and fulfilling life in one of the most beautiful places on the planet.

John and Sandra

They are a couple who could have retired wherever they liked. Compared to all of our other interviewees, they are loaded. Even though any retirement destination was wide open for them, they chose Bali.

They bought a twenty-year lease with extension options on an existing property in Seminyak, the bustling core village of expat life. Their place might be described as Euro-Bali, not the thatched-roof look but a slick, sexy marble and stone two-storey, with all bedrooms and living areas opening onto an expansive deck fronting an infinity pool. There is the sound of a waterfall somewhere on the property, which has a view that overlooks rice paddies and rainforest.

"The most cathartic thing we have ever done is to sell our home and everything else—the lot—back in 2005 and then move to Bali," John said.

"There is a huge expatriate community here, a large social group to bond with," Sandra said. "We have a whole set of great new friends from all over the world ranging in age from thirty-five to eighty-five. And they are all here for different reasons and do very different things."

Referring to the array of foreign cultures and lifestyles and the differing financial circumstances that make up the intriguing character of the country, John said, "Bali is like a multi-layered cake. Something for everybody. It suits us. I don't miss my old life at all and I have no interest in going back to it. And our children and friends simply love visiting us here."

Before buying, it is wise to rent to ensure you understand the area, the legal system, the local values, and, indeed, whether it is worth buying at all rather than renting at very low cost and keeping your nest egg intact.

PROPERTY

Relative to Canada, buying property in Bali is still inexpensive, but the ownership structure can be complicated. This is a country where quality legal advice, which is readily available, is critically important. And before buying it is wise to rent to ensure you understand the area, the legal system, the community, and, indeed, whether it is worth buying at all. It is important to note that renting long term in Bali is a bargain—lovely, centrally located three-bedroom pool villas go for $2,000 a month or less.

The major complication to property ownership is important to understand. A non-Indonesian citizen *cannot* own freehold property—land, villas, houses, or apartments—outright in Indonesia. (See Bali Property in chapter 11 for details.)

However, a foreigner can acquire a leasehold title to a property. This is almost the same as a *strata title* except this title lasts for only twenty-five years (or less), with an extension of thirty years negotiable (the government is considering extending this up to seventy years). Then the property reverts to the original owner (lessor).

Lease periods vary but the leases themselves are flexible. They can be bought or sold or sublet just the same as freehold property.

Many foreigners still insist on freehold ownership in the belief it protects and ensures their investment long term. They can engineer this in one of two ways: they can use an Indonesian nominee on the title or set up an Indonesian company to hold the title. Thousands of expat villa owners have used the nominee system. Lawyers and property agents are adept at setting you up. But using a nominee is clearly seen by the government as a way to circumvent the law. While this strategy is common, buyers should be fully aware that, in any dispute or if property law changes, their name is *not* on the title, and they should expect no sympathy in an Indonesian court if there is an issue.

Leases are the safest way of holding property in Indonesia because they do not involve an effort to circumvent the law using freehold nominees. Buying a long-term leasehold does not require participation of a nominee.

Once you get past this rather large hurdle, the process of purchasing or leasing a property is quite simple. Bali has a sophisticated, foreigner-friendly real estate industry. Well-known expat-run agencies like Ray White, Century 21, or Knight Frank/Elite Havens are there to provide guidance to expats.

Geoffrey and Michael are completely comfortable with their leasing deal and don't see the lack of clear freehold ownership as a major problem. Geoffrey compares it to the leasing situation he is familiar with in London. "To buy a property in most areas of the City of London requires the purchase of a lease, not the freehold title," he explained. "You can sell the lease, rent it out, leave it to your family, whatever." If Indonesian authorities do lengthen the maximum extension period to seventy years from thirty years, leaseholds will be even more attractive. This change has been openly discussed by the government, and usually action follows when things get that kind of public exposure.

The increased demand for properties in Bali over the last decade has triggered some steep price increases, particularly in high-demand areas. Not surprisingly, Bali has seen the sharpest rise in land values in all of Indonesia. According to research conducted by Knight Frank/Elite Havens, average land prices increased 34 per cent throughout 2011 and luxury estate prices jumped another 20 per cent in 2012.

That is high, but in some areas the escalation is even greater. Land prices near the desirable beaches in Seminyak (like Legian, Petitenget, and Batu Belig) rose 50 to 87 per cent in 2011. Knight Frank/Elite Havens says these huge increases are driven by investors building rental villas in very high-demand areas. However, compared to Canada's more preferred locations, property is still quite cheap. An attractive three- to four-bedroom with pool villa can be purchased on a twenty-year lease with extensions for $250,000 in popular Seminyak or up the coast a mile or two in trendy Canggu. The further away from the beach-tourism hot zones you go, the cheaper it becomes. In the central Ubud region, prices for the same sort of property start at $100,000. Last I looked, that gets you an old outhouse in Muskoka, and it doesn't come with a pool. It is important to keep up to date on Bali real estate costs. The massive overbuilding may soon reach a point where there is more inventory than buyers. It's not strongly evident yet, but there are signs of slowing demand.

However, there is another way to find accommodation.

The Bali building boom has seen many hundreds—in fact, a few thousand—villas built in every corner of the island. Many, if not most, are rental properties, and the rest are pretty much unoccupied by their owners outside of key holiday periods of the year. To be sure, Christmas, New Year's, and Chinese New Year's command high rents and high occupancies. However, in our experience, that may well be the only rental income many places get for the year. Enter long-term rental. We have seen properties in Seminyak, just off the beach, that rent for $5,000 a week at Christmas that will rent on a twelve-month basis for $2,000 *a month!* That is a new, furnished top to bottom, three-bedroom pool villa complete with daily maid service, gardeners, and security within a few minutes' walk from the best shops and restaurants on the island. In Ubud, a similar rental can be had for $1,000 a month—just $12,000 a year! The owners do ask for all the rental fee up front, but it is Bali and everything is negotiable. In any case, we strongly support the idea of renting before you buy or build, and this is the best way to test drive the island in comfort before you commit your money to a long-term purchase.

Annie

Annie is a Canadian from Winnipeg. She came to Bali in her 20s to hang out with friends of her family who had a grand old home in Batu Belig. She never left.

Now, a dozen years later, she sells residential real estate for one of the best expat-run companies here. When we first met her years ago, she was selling a lot of gated compound residences. But there were problems with permits and financing that delayed or even stopped some construction. Now her company sells mainly stand-alone built properties or undeveloped land all over the island.

Her view on Bali is unhesitating and refreshingly direct.

"Bali either sucks you in or spits you out," she said. We must have looked surprised because she gave us a "let me explain" smile. "I believe in karma. If you disrespect the locals and their customs and create drama, it will spit you out. But, if you embrace the spirit of this place, you may never want to leave."

Annie acknowledged there are a few ongoing issues and that the booming investment and population increases have stretched island resources.

"Medical would be the number one deterrent to retiring in Bali," Annie said. "The fact that foreign doctors are not allowed to practise here is a long-standing problem that just doesn't go away. And the water shortage is real. In some areas like the Bukit in the southwest that were built on limestone, there is barely any well water at all. Hundreds of villas and dozens of hotels must bring water in by tanker. Electricity just went up 25 per cent across the island as subsidies came off, and gasoline went up as well. We had to adjust office salaries to accommodate it."

We suggested these issues seem rather serious. She agreed, but it hasn't put her off living in Bali.

She shook her head at the thought. "No. Not a bit. I can't imagine leaving." Clearly Annie isn't going anywhere. At least not back to Canada or winter, she says.

"You do need to get out of the hustle of Seminyak when you can. On the weekends there are so many wonderful places to go, such as over to the neighbouring island of Lombok off the East Coast or to the Gili Islands for diving. Even here in Bali, you can go up north into the mountains or to the quiet beaches on the north shore where it can still be just as pristine as it was thirty years ago."

It appears Annie has her Muskoka/Sunshine Coast/Laurentian–like weekend retreats right here at home.

"Bali either sucks you in or spits you out. If you disrespect the locals, their religion and customs, it will spit you out. But respect the spirit of the place and you may never want to leave."

COST OF LIVING

Living well is cheap in Bali but just how cheap depends on the lifestyle you want to have. If you want to enjoy the high life, you can do it for a lot less than you can in a Western country.

The rather well-to-do Sandra said, "The food is exquisite and cheap. We buy export quality, sashimi-grade tuna for ten dollars a kilo. A dinner party around the pool for thirty is common as it is so affordable." Added John, "I have a ninety-minute massage three times a week for ten dollars a session. We have six staff and they cost about a hundred dollars a month each. They take care of the house, the pool, the shopping, the cooking, the driving, the security, etc. We don't need to lift a finger."

He conceded that Bali has become more expensive in the last few years, and "there are issues about good medical services and electricity costs have soared." His biggest gripe is the cost of a bottle of wine as a 300 per cent import tax is applied. Recently, Australian winemakers have been planting shaded vines in Bali, producing very decent wines that escape the duty. They also bring in Aussie grapes from Western Australia's Margaret River in bulk concentrate; when aged and bottled locally, those very drinkable whites, reds, and rosés escape the duty as well. For liquor, though, there's no solution. Learn to love beer and wine or make that gin and tonic a special-occasion choice.

Not all expats in Bali are as affluent as John and Sandra. It is a different story for Michael and Geoffrey in Ubud, who

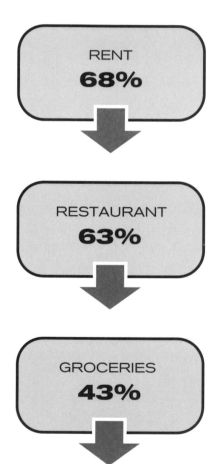

COST OF LIVING

INDICES
BALI lower than **TORONTO**

RENT
68%

RESTAURANT
63%

GROCERIES
43%

Source: numbeo.com

have to be more careful with their limited funds. Even so, they live a life of relative luxury with three employees who tend the house and gardens and take care of security. Their three staff cost them just $200 a month total. The housekeeper comes in the mornings and prepares breakfast, makes beds, cleans bathrooms, does laundry and dishes, and will prepare their evening meal. The gardener comes every morning as well, cleaning the pool and taking care of the grounds. This leaves their afternoons as a nice private time until the security guard comes from dusk to dawn.

"It's a good idea to have security," said Michael. "They are local people and, in a sense, that guarantees you are safe from break-ins and petty theft. If you don't have them, it's pretty much an invitation to an occasional robbery. Still, this is petty crime, which happens everywhere, and you just have to be as aware as you are at home."

In Bali, more and larger Western supermarkets like Carrefour are opening. New restaurants seem to appear weekly, and since eating out is considered very much part of local life, expats revel in the wide choice on offer—at minimal cost.

Dining out at an inexpensive restaurant costs about a quarter of what it would at home. At a *warung*, a local restaurant, you can get a meal for less than $5. For example, fried noodles, lemongrass chicken, fresh green beans, a chicken satay, and a spring roll is about three bucks. Add a frosty local Bintang beer for a dollar.

Not only is the food very cheap, the quality is excellent. For breakfast you can order a healthy egg-white omelet with mushrooms and tomatoes, two slices of wholegrain toast, fresh mango juice, and yogurt with fruit and granola for $3. The delicious local Balinese coffee is a steal at just 25 cents a cup. Of course, you can always go to a high-end tourist spot like Grocer & Grind for lattes and cappuccinos but, at less than $3 a cup, still only pay half the price you pay at home.

If you prefer dining in, the savings are also massive—especially if you shop at the local markets and not the supermarket. The *pasar*, or local market, has fresh vegetables and fruit for pennies but a little bargaining is called for to get a local price. Even in the supermarkets with fixed prices, you will find groceries are 50 per cent lower in Bali than they are at home.

As well as saving on food, you no longer have to rely on buses and trains to get around. A local Blue Bird taxi, on a meter, is 20 per cent of the cost of a cab ride in downtown Toronto. The cost of utilities (even electricity, which locals think is pricey) is 40 per cent lower than most of Canada and, when you factor in the low cost of rent, you are living for much less and living very well.

That said, some Western items are priced close to what they are in Canada. A pair of Levi jeans or a new VW Golf will be at least as much as or more than at home, and that frothy cappuccino can cost ten times the price of a local coffee. The bars and restaurants just off the beaches that cater to tourists, like the very swish La Lucciola in Seminyak, will cost you almost as much as you would pay on Queen Street or Robson Street. But add a bottle of fine, imported Italian Chianti with the 300 per cent duty and it will actually cost you more.

Dining out in an inexpensive local restaurant costs 80 per cent less in Bali than in a decent coffee shop in Toronto. Add a beer for a dollar.

Although you might consider buying a car, drivers in Bali are pretty much crazy everywhere and absolutely insane in the

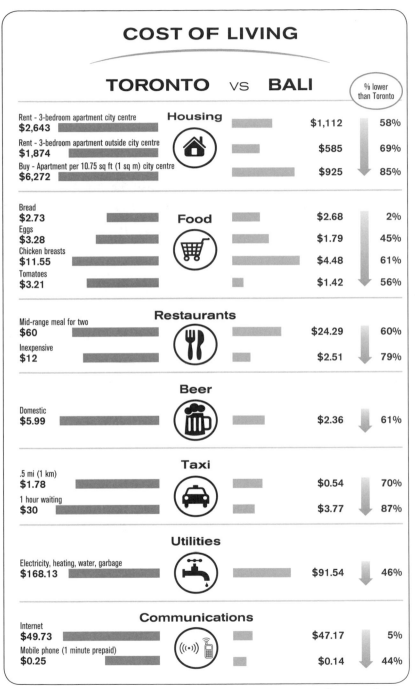

COST OF LIVING

TORONTO vs BALI

% lower than Toronto

Housing

	Toronto	Bali	% lower
Rent - 3-bedroom apartment city centre	$2,643	$1,112	58%
Rent - 3-bedroom apartment outside city centre	$1,874	$585	69%
Buy - Apartment per 10.75 sq ft (1 sq m) city centre	$6,272	$925	85%

Food

	Toronto	Bali	% lower
Bread	$2.73	$2.68	2%
Eggs	$3.28	$1.79	45%
Chicken breasts	$11.55	$4.48	61%
Tomatoes	$3.21	$1.42	56%

Restaurants

	Toronto	Bali	% lower
Mid-range meal for two	$60	$24.29	60%
Inexpensive	$12	$2.51	79%

Beer

	Toronto	Bali	% lower
Domestic	$5.99	$2.36	61%

Taxi

	Toronto	Bali	% lower
.5 mi (1 km)	$1.78	$0.54	70%
1 hour waiting	$30	$3.77	87%

Utilities

	Toronto	Bali	% lower
Electricity, heating, water, garbage	$168.13	$91.54	46%

Communications

	Toronto	Bali	% lower
Internet	$49.73	$47.17	5%
Mobile phone (1 minute prepaid)	$0.25	$0.14	44%

Source: numbeo.com

hectic south. Roads are impossibly narrow and poorly marked with few lights at night. Better to find a car rental company with a driver you can access as required. If you simply must have your own car, make sure you have an international driving permit and the very best insurance you can buy. Car prices are slightly more than they are in the Canada but don't even consider a big SUV. Some two-lane roads are so narrow even one SUV wouldn't fit!

As for those cute little scooters you can rent for $5 a day, you should know that motorbike accidents are the number one cause of death in Bali. Denpasar's Sanglah Hospital treats 150 accident victims a day, every day. The number can hit *300 a day* over a weekend. Check your insurance; although the driver may be covered, the passenger is not. And as for the bike itself, none of it is insured. Bend it—you pay for it.

Officially, there were 1.5 million scooters on Bali roads in 2010, and more were being added at the rate of 500 a day. That adds up to more than 2 million scooters and motorcycles now clogging the narrow roads, creating a mind-numbing gridlock morning and night that catches up more than a few foreigners who aren't used to the aggressive, no-rules driving habits. It is interesting to us that people who have never been on a scooter in their life think that learning on the roads of Bali is a wise choice.

Here's a tip: Don't.

Take a cab. Blue Bird taxis are all over the island and they will happily wait for you while you pick up your Aussie beef tenderloin at the Bali Deli for tonight's BBQ.

MEDICAL SERVICES

Southeast Asian governments and private investment partners see a whole new industry emerging. They have watched the surge in medical tourism in Bangkok and Penang. There, you get world-class medical care in facilities that are practically resort quality at prices that are a fraction of the costs in the West.

Contrast that with those in Canada on provincial medical care without expensive, private top-ups. You can wait for months for critical services in stretched facilities with a bedside manner you might once have described as third world.

What if the new third-world medical services are becoming, as we suggest, what the first world should have been? And consider that retirement tourism, a completely logical extension, is around the corner.

Bali is just beginning to join this new age of Asian service industries in both medical care and planned retirement. They are late on both fronts, and the promise is far from the reality, so far. The name of their key retiree program is a bit of a mouthful: Creating Retirement Tourism in Bali: Retire in Paradise.

Sponsored by the government with private investors, the aim is to provide sixteen private self-contained gated communities with attached Western medical facilities staffed by Western doctors. The first of these will be up and running in 2015, and the plan is to be servicing many thousands of people by 2020. As in all things Bali, that fixed date is give or take a few years. Doing things on time—or as promised—is not a Balinese strong point. They have one word, *besok*, that—tellingly—means tomorrow, next week, next month, or next year.

Hopefully, though, this new initiative will be a part-answer to long-held concerns about the quality of Bali medical care. Although basic needs have been met, serious illness or trauma has usually required expensive evacuation to Singapore or Bangkok. Today in Bali, many new clinics and hospitals have opened on the island—places like private Australian-run BIMC Hospitals in Kuta and Nusa Dua and the main public hospital, Sanglah, in Denpasar, which now offers an international wing with costly VIP and Super VIP care. However, they are still not nearly up to Thailand or Singapore levels. Bali medical care seriously lags behind its more sophisticated neighbours' high standards. Why? Some of the facilities may be new, but the quality of medical services and staff remains suspect. Expats say the single biggest reason for this is that foreign (read Western) doctors are not allowed to practise in Indonesia. Observe in some cases, but not practise.

If you can afford medical insurance, get it. What happens if you have a car or a motorcycle accident or get a life-threatening illness? The medical help in Bali may not be adequate and you will need to travel or, in the worst case, be evacuated to Singapore or Thailand for proper treatment.

Ian

Ian is a hotel manager. Not just a regular GM, he is regarded as one of the best on the island. The gorgeous all-villa property facing Seminyak Beach that he has run for eight years is picture-perfect, with over 80 per cent occupancy year round. Considering that overbuilt Bali in January 2014 had a hotel occupancy rate of 56 per cent, his five-star care shows.

Ian left the United Kingdom when his kids were in university. After years of teaching hospitality in London and working in hotel management posts in the Caribbean, he came to Bali.

"I wish I had done it years ago," Ian said. "I find life simple here, no stress. Everything is done for you. I like to wash my own car. It's just a thing I enjoy. I can't even bring out the hose and it's being done for me. The local people are wonderful, they make all the difference to life here.

"Bali is like a small village in England. It's an island, small, community driven, and easy to navigate. Not that you walk a lot here like in London or Singapore. I find it too hot, even on the beach with a breeze off the ocean."

Ian owns two homes. One is in Seminyak, where he lives, and the other is down the coast, where he hopes to retire. As he is married to an Indonesian, purchasing property was easy. No nominee required.

He finds that, so far, Australians are the most prevalent group of expats in Bali. Most, he says, split the year between Bali and Australia. There are lots of Americans, too, he says. And Brits and French as well.

I wonder about Canadians. Not that many. Not yet anyway.

Although Ian works and lives in bustling Seminyak, he knows the entire island well after so many years in residence. "Ubud is the place to relax, Candi Dasa on the east coast is in the middle-growth stage, and just a few miles north is Canggu. It is the Seminyak of tomorrow; it is twice as expensive as Ubud already."

He has experience with Bali medical services and it hasn't been good. "I had a swelling in my neck that spread to my face. I went to the new BIMC Australian-owned-and-operated hospital, saw a local doctor, and they gave me their usual treatment of antibiotics. Symptoms got worse. Someone told me about a Chinese doctor running a small clinic in Denpasar. In a brief but thorough exam, he told me it wasn't an infection; it was most likely cancer. He gave me three choices: go to Perth, Singapore, or Bangkok—immediately, as in the next day. I chose Mount Elizabeth Hospital in Singapore, who confirmed I had stage four lymphoma, and I started treatment within hours. Nine months of chemo cost me over $20,000 and now my medical insurance is $15,000 a year!"

Ian believes that not allowing foreign doctors to practise in Bali is the direct cause of his misdiagnosis. Finding the Chinese doctor was just lucky, but his own medical experience hasn't changed his positive opinion of Bali. He finally sees a real effort being made both by government and private means to correct the environmental wrongs of the past decade. For years, Ian and his fellow hoteliers on Seminyak Beach had been forced to clean the 1.8 miles (3 kilometres) of public beach themselves with local hired labour every day of the year on morning and evening tides. The island's government has now provided two tractor-driven mechanical beach cleaners that run seven days a week.

"It's a start," he said. "To me Bali is still mystical, magical, spiritual. I lead a stress-free and simple, full life here. Many things have changed—that has not."

> *To me Bali is still mystical, magical, and spiritual. I live a stress-free and simple, full life here. Many things have changed—that has not.*

There is no question that Bali has its issues. Some will be solved and some will not. Medical care is improving but too slowly; the mounting garbage problem has been identified in everything from *The Wall Street Journal* to *Le Monde* and can be fixed if the government takes heed. The unrestricted development seems to be getting under better control, and infrastructure is improving even if not fast enough to match the rapid growth. There is a new airport in Denpasar and a new east-west expressway, and new catchments and reservoirs are planned to capture and recycle the significant rainfall in monsoon season. New power plants have been proposed, and cleaning up the beaches is now a priority. Bali needs to prove they can get these things done.

THE SPIRITUAL SIDE

There are many positive elements of Bali and island culture that are deeply spiritual and strongly community centred. As a result, the Balinese people are among the kindest and most caring in Asia. Bali is divided into regencies (like provinces) and further subdivided down to villages. Each village is a model of a traditional co-operative society where all ages are respected, all points of view valued. The Balinese are exemplary as service staff, and every resident expat is required by their visa to engage at least one *pembantu*, generally a maid or housekeeper, but they provide so many more services. They will shop, cook, clean, pay bills, manage your property, and care for your every need—and for as little as $100 a month. They are also wonderful caregivers for older expats as *pembantu* are naturally respectful, patient, and gentle. If your particular health requirements require professional help, hiring a full-time nurse is in the range of $300 to $600 a month depending on the caregiver's local or international qualifications.

You have to ask if our Canadian support services are any better than this. And then ask if the centuries-old Balinese culture of caring for people as you would your own family isn't better still. Much better.

Paulo and Isotta

We met and interviewed Paulo and Isotta in a café less than a block from their store in Seminyak. These Italians came to Bali fourteen years ago as visitors and never left. In their stylish boutique, they sell their own designs of luscious, contemporary silk hand-made clothing—everything from full-length gowns to flowing pants and halter tops. They collaborate on the designs and have a factory in Ubud. They keep homes in both places. Although they sell in Seminyak, they prefer to live in Ubud.

Isotta says, "In Ubud there is a sense of community. You feel the spirit and culture of Bali. And there is always something wonderful going on. They celebrated the tenth year of the Ubud Writers and Readers Festival in 2013. The BaliSpirit Festival is held there every year in March. It's a global celebration of yoga, dance, and music. Even down here in Kuta they have events like Balinale, a film festival held every November."

They both have enthusiastically embraced Balinese culture. Paulo spoke of it: "A person in Bali cannot exist alone. The society is very community based … organized around a *banjar* [village compound]. Every week there is a religious event of some kind where they all participate. Balinese are used to being part of a group and taking care of each other. This spills over to you if you let it. You are part of their lives and vice versa—especially older people that they see as their responsibility to look after."

Isotta added, "Everything is discussed and resolved as much as possible at the village level. They find solutions that make everyone happy. Compromise here is a good thing."

With a smile, they both admitted it took time for the locals to get used to an Italian temperament. They were stunned at the Italian way of communicating: loudly. They explained that they rarely see fights or yelling or expressions of negative emotions because the Balinese are taught all their lives to be in harmony with their surroundings.

"It was a challenge," Paulo said, "for us to adjust to their culture at first, their way of working, too. You need to be careful to interpret their different version of the truth. The Balinese value of honesty is different than the West. They don't want to lose face above all things, and sometimes lying or denying is the best response when aggressively confronted. They don't give criticism in their culture but they don't accept it well either. We've learned over the years to read the nuances of their ways, and now it works very well for us."

Neither Paulo nor Isotta have much experience with the local medical community as their Italian citizenship allows them to maintain their Italian health care wherever they live, however long they live away from Italy and assuming they can get home to Italy. Nice perk. They do suggest that while they feel care in Bali is adequate, they have heard of long waits for specialist consultations and treatments. They have been told that local doctors usually load patients up with antibiotics; cortisone is prescribed for every ailment.

Both have been on renewable tourist visas since they arrived fourteen years ago. Paulo says, "Simple. First rule is you don't do it yourself. There are good immigration agents who do it for you, and do-it-yourself is a little bit frowned upon as you are taking that job from someone else."

They both feel life on Bali has been very good for them.

"We don't really have many close Balinese friends," said Paulo. "Some [of those we've become friends with] have studied abroad, have good English, and are more Western."

Isotta quickly added, "But we do happily engage with local people every day: our store staff, our factory workers, suppliers, customers, the people in the markets. They know us there. I can get anything I want in the markets: Japanese, Italian. And the Balinese in-home massages we have at least every week are wonderful and so cheap."

Like everyone who works in a downtown core anywhere in the world, even people in Bali feel the pressure sometimes. "We do feel the need to get away from the hyper-development of Bali—especially here in Seminyak. You can still find serenity on the island but you need to go east from here or north."

They both like getting off the island occasionally.

"We just got back from the island of Flores," said Paulo. "The flight is $80 each, and for three days it only costs $130 for lodging and food. The beaches are beautiful there. Lovely crystal-clear water with great diving and snorkelling."

I asked what makes Bali so special for them.

Paulo answered. "This place has a unique energy. It's magical and so too the beauty of the people, who are so peaceful and charming. I'm never stressed out here. No issues with taxes or visas. As a small-business owner I work with wonderful craftsmen in silk, wood, metal, and stone who create beautiful things for and with me. Everyone is open, accepting, tolerant. They will gladly teach you and involve you in their culture. We love that."

We met with Paulo and Isotta the day before Nyepi, the Balinese New Year that occurs following the dark moon of the spring equinox (around March 31 for those who don't have their Balinese Hindu calendars handy).

It is the most sacred of the many Hindu holidays and very different from the usual lively religious celebrations. Known in English as the Day of Silence, it commences at six a.m. and concludes at six a.m. the following day. As the name implies, for a period of twenty-four hours all of Bali is silent. There are no planes in or out, no cars or motorbikes, no bars or restaurants open, no music playing, no one on the streets or on the beaches. Lights are dimmed and any food consumed is prepared the day before. There is no work, no play. It is a day reserved for self-reflection and meditation. Only *pecalungs* (village wardens), in their black hats and checkerboard wraps, patrol the empty streets and beaches ensuring everyone, including tourists, respects the silence.

Hotels get a partial exemption, but there are no keg parties around the pool. The next day the partying resumes in earnest with mass parades and festivals all over the island.

Paulo and Isotta have fallen under the spell of the spirituality of Bali culture. They started mediating with a local guru in 2010 and it changed their lives.

As Isotta told us, "I have never been able to just sit quietly without thinking. [Meditation] has been life-transforming for both of us in our business partnership and our personal relationship. It got us through a business crisis in late 2010 where we both needed to calm our minds down, and now we help each other through our journey."

VISAS AND IMMIGRATION

One of the most common topics for Bali expats is, "What visa are you on?" A number of visa options are available so you can probably find one that will suit your circumstances and needs.

All foreigners entering Bali get a tourist visa. A visa on arrival (VOA) is valid for thirty days and can be extended to sixty. After sixty days, if you want to extend your time in Bali, you must exit the country and re-enter—locals call it a visa run—and it is the most common type of visa in use. (Recently, Bali removed its paid "visa on arrival" requirement for 35 countries, including Canada. That only saves you $35 but as much as 2 to 4 hours in the dreaded visa line-up.)

A retirement or renewable stay visa is available to those over 55 years of age who can prove they have an income of at least $18,000 a year. Applicants must also show proof of health insurance in either their own country or Indonesia. They must agree to employ an Indonesian maid, not to work locally, and show proof of accommodation that is either rented for at least $500 a month or purchased for at least $35,000.

The visa is for one year but can be renewed annually in-country up to a maximum of five years. After that, it is possible to apply for a permanent stay visa. (See chapter 10 for more details.)

Tips and Traps: Bali

1. Rent before you buy. With gorgeous villas renting for less than $2,000 a month on a one-year lease, you may not want to ever buy.

2. Although housing is still cheap relative to Canada, ownership can be complicated, and freehold requires the legal engineering of an Indonesian nominee on the title.

3. Health care and medical services in Bali are still marginal. They are adequate for basic needs but not for anything major no matter how nicely they gloss things over with fancy new facilities.

4. Medical insurance and evacuation insurance is a must-have if you have any serious medical issues, especially for people over 65.

5. The cost of living can be cheap as chips if you go local. It is very affordable, as much as 50 to 60 per cent less than Canada. For that you can have a quality of life at least as good as home, and, of course, five star–plus in Bali is simply fantastic.

FINAL THOUGHT

As mentioned, we've been to Bali 14 times in 8 years. And while we were writing this book, we booked a small beach villa for Chinese New Year's. Our fifteenth visit. There is just something about the place that pulls you back. However, it is paradise with problems. They can all be solved, but the government has to enforce existing development codes and step up their infrastructure investment. So far, they have not done nearly enough. We think Bali is best suited to either a younger crowd or the more well-heeled who can buy their way out of infrastructure issues.

As a vacation spot, it is still fabulous. If you are in your 40s and want a life change, this is the place for you. However, as a retirement destination for Canadian retirees in their 60s it lacks the quality services, particularly health care, that you would find in Thailand or Malaysia.

THE CHECKLIST

1. The cost of living is low but housing can take it as high as you want. Stay away from the heavily congested tourist areas that charge Western prices. Local food and local restaurants are very cheap. Thumbs mostly up.
2. Property buying is not easy. It is complicated. Buying a condo or apartment is easier but very few are built for expats yet. Renting long term is a bargain. Thumbs up only for renting.
3. Health care is basic despite the fancy-looking new facilities. Generally speaking, all Indonesian health care is just about the worst in Asia. If you have a serious medical problem, you might need to be evacuated, so medical evacuation insurance is a wise purchase. Thumbs down.
4. Short-term visas of thirty days plus a thirty-day renewal are the most common. Longer-term visas are possible. Use an agent. Thumbs partly up.

Thailand

chapter 4

Thailand:
The Land of Smiles

The Thais call their country the Land of Smiles. It is not an exaggeration. Cultured, historic, and exotic under one all-encompassing, azure-blue sky. The beaches are epic—what tropical beaches are supposed to be. The cities are a mix of spectacular, ancient golden temples but bursting with new, first-world architecture and technology. The entire country is under the gentle spell of Buddhism, a religion in which even ancient banyan tree trunks are wrapped in sacred cloth to honour the modesty of their resident spirits.

And the food! One of the finest menus in all Asia, Thai cooking incorporates the four fundamental flavours of sweet, salty, sour, and spicy in myriad dishes to suit every taste. Just like the country itself, there is something for everybody here.

GETTING TO KNOW THAILAND

The incredible variety of this country is revealed via a slightly larger landmass than Spain with over 64 million people, 95 per cent of whom are Theraveda Buddhist, probably the most peaceful, quietest, and least invasive of all religions in Asia. On its northern border are Laos and Myanmar, to the east is Cambodia, to the south is the Gulf of Thailand and Malaysia. The west coast faces the gorgeous Andaman Sea with the beaches of Phuket and Krabi on one side and the island of Koh Samui sitting out in the Gulf on the other. Thailand has a varied tropical climate with three seasons rather than the usual two. The dry season is October to February, and the wet season is May to September. A shorter third season (we will just call it hot) is March to May.

We have been to Thailand half a dozen times, visiting the cities of Bangkok and Chiang Mai and the island and beach resorts on the Andaman Sea. The country has always been one of our favourite destinations and offers great advantages to a Canadian retiree. It is inexpensive, the people are lovely, the climate superb (if you like it hot), the health care services excellent, and the choice of places to live plentiful and diverse.

The political system in Thailand, however, is certainly different than almost anything you have ever known. From an outsider's perspective, fuelled by dramatic Western news coverage, it can at times look chaotic. To us who live in the region, it is uniquely Thai. The country has a revered royal family and, most of the time, a working democracy. The issue is that it's a political quagmire interrupted rather regularly by military *coups d'états*. But a coup in Thailand is very different to one you might read about in South America or Africa.

There have been eleven successful and seven unsuccessful coups since 1932. That total of eighteen is just short of the twenty-five general elections held in the same time period. Democracy is winning, barely.

The coup mentality stems from the polarization between the worker classes (red-shirted protesters) and the wealthy aristocrats (yellow-shirted protesters). Since the yellows have the money, they tend to win elections, prompting the reds to take to the streets. The latest coup was in May 2014. No one was killed, and life continued as usual for most people as nothing much had changed except the traffic was worse. When the military coup did come, most citizens welcomed it since, as usual, it brought an end to six months of political stalemate. There will no doubt be fresh elections after a period of stabilization when Thailand's booming economy regroups. Will there be more coups in the future? Likely. Once you've had a dozen successful coups, it becomes the default solution for settling things down—the equivalent of telling your kids to go to their room or, these days, take a time out.

We were in Bangkok during the last coup. It was a model of organization and ended quietly when it was rumoured the store owners in the malls asked politely if they could get back to the business of draining the tourists' pockets. It appeared to us rather more like an office picnic than a serious confrontation.

That said, it can get rowdy on the front lines and very occasionally it can get ugly. Protesters were killed in the 2010 coup when some army guys got out of hand and opened fire. Fortunately, this is a rare exception to the usual T-shirted reds and yellows waving flags, not guns, at each other. When it gets too heated, the much-revered King Bhumibol calls both sides in as he did in 2002. The two groups' leaders knelt before him and he said, "Enough." One word from him and it all ends.

For expat retirees, this is part of the Thai landscape and it really makes little day-to-day difference to them. Despite the frightening headlines in international newspapers, it is only politically active Thais who are affected. The traffic is a little worse but the demonstrations are all pretty much concentrated in areas where the traffic is always horrible anyway. Take the MRT subway to get around. It's excellent.

BANGKOK

The locals call it City of Angels but that is just the first three words of the longest place name in the world—there are twenty-eight more words in the description. Here it is:

> City of angels, great city of immortals, magnificent city of the nine gems, seat of the King, city of royal palaces, home of the God's incarnate, erected by Visvakarman at Indra's behest.

That little beauty is taught to every schoolchild and then promptly forgotten, much like my high school Latin. That is Bangkok. It's as complicated as its name.

The city is a study in contrasts. On the one hand, it is full of astonishingly beautiful temples, amazing history, spectacular hotels, wonderful restaurants, and some of the best shopping in Asia. On the other, it is also the Asian HQ for the sex trade, with the infamous Patpong Road leading the charge. Here, there are over one hundred bars full of willing girls and katoeys, the famous Thai "ladyboys" who will both shock and amaze you. A little less in your face (so to speak) is the Soi Cowboy district, where there are more than thirty ladyboy bars conveniently located right across the street from Terminal 21, the newest, most spectacular shopping mall in Bangkok.

Bangkok now beats Paris as the number one tourist destination in the world, with just under 16 million foreign visitors in 2013; that's five times what the entire island of Bali gets. Situated in the Chao Praya River Delta, the city is crisscrossed by ancient canals, defeating any kind of road grid system. Traffic is horrible at all times of the day, making the aforementioned MRT transit system a great alternative to the roads. It has four lines running and more under construction. Public transit not for you? You can take one of the more than 100,000 taxis or 56,000 licensed motorbike taxis if baking in traffic is your thing.

Mitchell

Mitchell is a Canadian who works for an NGO (non-government organization) that is one of the world's largest charities. In his late 40s, he had lived in Bangkok for three years when we interviewed him. While far from retirement himself, he has a good sense of the place, its strengths, its weaknesses, and, above all, its cost of living from his years of experience at postings all over Southeast Asia.

"I find Bangkok cheap and cheerful. The Thai people are extremely friendly and courteous. They are motivated and hard-working even if they work in ways that Westerners find a bit confusing."

Mitchell explained, "In a restaurant, food comes when it is cooked, not in any kind of sequence that you ordered. And it will never, ever all come at the same time. So eat whatever arrives, as the next dish may be a minute away or ten. It all does come eventually and it is almost always excellent, so just enjoy it."

Having lived all over Asia, Mitchell finds the cost of living in Bangkok very reasonable. "A big three-bedroom, three-bathroom of 200 square metres [2150 square feet], open concept with multiple balconies, can cost you as little as $1,500 a month. That is in a good neighbourhood. In a really great neighbourhood, you can get absolute five-star digs, but a little less space, for about the same amount."

Mitchell added, "There is a lot of building going on and, therefore, a lot of apartments and houses to choose from. I didn't consider buying as my job tends to have about a three-year run, and apartments, really great rental apartments, have worked fine for me."

He defines Bangkok costs in two categories.

"All things Thai (food, electronics, clothing, etc.) are incredibly inexpensive but Western goods are not. A Starbucks coffee costs about the same in Bangkok as it does in Toronto. Thai public transportation is *very* cheap but buying a car is not as cars are heavily taxed. However, all services that directly involve Thai people (maids, massages, gardeners, helpers, drivers, taxis) are shockingly cheap. You can get a daily maid who cleans and cooks for a hundred dollars a month."

He finds the city very safe. "Petty crime is minimal, and I have never felt threatened here in any way. I do suggest women need to be more aware of being out late at night as sex crimes do happen, even to Western women.'"

As for politics, he takes the economic view.

"Despite the protests and the occasional coup, I think this country will always be open for business. There is a huge amount of Japanese and, more recently, Chinese investment that tends to play a stabilizing role in the country. That money can, and occasionally does, get diverted to other low-cost Southeast Asian countries like Malaysia when political protests here drag on for too long. The people want to work, the government needs them to, the investment people insist on stability, and that is the case whoever is in power. When the present King dies, no doubt it will be a bit of a crisis, but I think the country is prepared for it and will pull through the transition of power to the Crown Prince."

Mitch has a few important words of advice for expats coming to Bangkok. "Sign up for thaivisaforum.com at least a month before you arrive. It will help you understand how things work here. Stick to your budget—it is so cheap, in your first few months you can easily overspend on gorgeous art, custom furniture, and sexy appliances. I did. And don't kid yourself, you will never speak perfect Thai and certainly not read or write it. A few key words go a long way."

> "When the present King dies, no doubt
> there will be a bit of a crisis, but I think
> the country will pull through the transition
> of power to the Crown Prince."

As for staying long term, Mitchell said, "Absolutely! Inexpensive to live, great food, super climate, and a ton of vacation destinations to go to all over the country. What's not to love?

"Thailand," he explained, "is like a buffet of lifestyle choices. You can live in a villa on the beach that would rank among the best in the world or live a bit inland in a Thai timber house nestled deep in a garden of exotic plants half the size of maple trees. There are high-end condominiums and apartments in the cities with every modern convenience you can possibly think of."

Not like Canada? He shook his head and smiled.

"You do not lack options here," he told me.

"In Thailand, and indeed Southeast Asia generally, you distinctly sense much more personal freedom than exists at home. Some find this lack of a nanny-state mentality uplift-ing, if a little foreign to our strict rule-based society. If you want to ride a motorbike without a helmet, then that's fine. If you want to jaywalk or go against the traffic lights, that's fine. If you want to have a beer with your kids and they are under 18, that's fine. If you don't want to wear a seat belt, then that's fine too."

But, he added, don't get caught doing something wrong in the eyes of the law. He told me that while there is a sense of much greater personal freedom in places like Thailand, there are actually far fewer legal rights, the opposite of what life is like at home.

Mitch made the point clearly: "It is important to keep in mind that, for things like property disputes or traffic accidents or even visa overstays, the fact that you believe you are clearly 100 per cent in the right is no guarantee you will ever win the argument." He added, "The reality is that experienced expats usually settle all kinds of disputes in cash at the side of the road, and it seems to be tantamount to bribery to the unini-tiated. It is not. Biting your tongue and paying some cash up front can save you from an endless and costly process where your chances of winning are slim to none."

PHUKET

If you dream about crystal-clear waters and powder-sand beaches, Thailand has a long list of choices for you. An hour and a bit flight time from Bangkok will put you in the thick of it, on the island of Phuket.

The locals say Phuket (the *h* is silent) comes from the words *phu* (mountain) and *ket* (jewel). Others believe it is a simple derivative of the Malay *bukit* (hill). Either way, it looks like a mountain from a distance, and it is a bit of a jewel even if a slightly tarnished one. It is a big island, about 30 per cent bigger than the island of Montreal. Driving south from the airport takes you to the island's west-coast hot spot, Patong, and its 1.8-mile-long (3-kilometre) beach.

This is ground zero for over 3 million foreign visitors a year who congregate on Bangla Road (for straight people) and Paradise Complex (for gays).

Larry

Larry was Australia's consul general in Phuket from 2005 to 2014. As in much of Southeast Asia, the Aussies here also look after Canadian interests as we do for them in other parts of the world.

Larry is a very plainspoken guy, and from his observations over the years, he doesn't feel Phuket is the best choice for a retiree. "I looked after fifty deaths a year—mostly Australians—half from natural causes and half from misadventure. Health insurance (or the lack of it) is a huge problem; location is another.

"A lot of people can only afford to live in the areas of Phuket that are not safe by Western standards," he said. "I am talking [about] in the south—even Thais don't like living down there. There are sea gypsies who are renowned housebreakers, [and there are] incidents of assault, robbery, and rape. The safety issue is a big one, and it comes from not having enough money to avoid living in the south. Fact is, with very reasonable finances, you don't ever have to go there. But thousands do."

Larry said extortion is rampant. For instance, he said young Thais on southern beaches will intentionally ram a rented personal watercraft with their own and then demand $5,000 to even $10,000 to cover the damage.

Another problem for Larry is that a lot of these marginal expat guys live in Patpong. It is sin city with a capital *S*, he said.

"We had one 55-year-old guy who thought he could make some money on the side selling a little bit of cocaine. Except he was selling it in an area where it's common knowledge the police have the cocaine concession. He got five years. He was lucky. If he was in Bali, dealing drugs is a death sentence at worst and a life sentence at best."

Massive personal freedoms and limited legal rights are a common theme in much of Southeast Asia. It is the opposite to Canada, where you may get a parking ticket but you have the right to fight it in court.

Sal and Glen

Sal and Glen have a much different point of view. They have lived in the south for more than five years; they own a café on the beach and have a gorgeous house not far from it. They love Phuket, love the south, and feel safe there.

The couple, both 65, retired to Thailand after half a lifetime in the wine and restaurant business. I asked Sal about their decision to move.

"I liked my life but we were ready to move on at 60. And, I got sick of being cold half the year."

I could certainly relate to that.

"We had come here on holiday several times. We liked it and thought a little café on the beach would be perfect for us.

We packed up a container, brought some of our furniture (just the pieces that mattered to us), and left nothing in storage. We had no plan to go home—this was it."

It's five years on. What about any regrets?

Sal said, "The only regret we have moving here is the grandchildren. They weren't yet born when we came here." But, as Sal pointed out, technology these days goes a long way toward overcoming the tyranny of distance. "I speak to them every day on Skype. When my granddaughter saw me at the airport last year she kept feeling my face to see if it was a real one rather than the one she knows on the screen."

Glen and Sal have a three-bedroom, three-bathroom house just off the beach with an infinity pool, a view of the water, and wonderful gardens. It would sell for around a quarter of a million dollars. They enjoy luxuries they could not have at home, such as a live-in maid who does everything for them for $300 a month. Eating out for restaurant people is a treat because they cook for a living. In Phuket, they eat out all the time, only cooking a big dinner of roast lamb at home for friends and family about once a month.

And, despite Larry's expressed concerns about the south of the island, they feel very safe.

"We don't see property theft as a big problem. We leave all the café outdoor tables and chairs outside every night and nobody touches them. I rarely lock up the house." He did warn, though, that there are some precautions foreigners should take. "Certainly, you don't want to put any Thai person seriously offside, especially if you are standing between him and a pile of money. But we are primarily retired and why would we ever do that?"

As for the island's ubiquitous sex tourism industry and how she copes, Sal said it is easily managed because some villages and towns are worse than others and can be simply avoided. "I have no problem going into a bar with foreign men and Thai girls. I think the girls are lovely. They come and talk to me. I give them advice if they ask. They call me mama. As for seedy Patpong, I never go—haven't been for years."

And why would she? The main street of Patpong is lined with sticky girlie bars and sweaty Thai boxing exhibitions. Neon signs flicker, cheap market stalls dot the seascape, and tourism seems dominated by leering middle-aged men. As Sal said, "Patpong sits in the sharpest of contrasts to the upmarket areas on the northwestern side of the island: Kamala Beach, Surin Beach, Bang Tao Beach, and Laguna Beach."

To me there is a little touch of Palm Springs in these very upscale areas. A little bit anyway.

In Phuket, residential life on the northwest side is quiet and dignified, offering a convenient and relaxing lifestyle. You can play golf at a gorgeous public course for less than $40 a round and another $7 for the required caddy (use of a caddy is required all over Asia). That is pretty affordable but just one of many public and private courses that dot the island. The Phuket Country Club is where expats go for fairway villa living in a gated golf community.

As for shopping and Western-style supplies, Sal said she can now get everything she needs at the local supermarket. "When we arrived five years ago, there were a lot of things that were not available but now you can get everything you want." At the local Villa Supermarket, she said, "I can get everything from Jiff-brand peanut butter to mint sauce for my lamb roasts to fresh rosemary and the most fragrant Thai basil that you could ever imagine."

In Phuket you can play golf at a gorgeous
course for less than $40 a round and another $7
for your very pretty caddy to help you around.

Phuket certainly has its bad parts (or good depending on your tastes). As we've heard, it isn't all rough trade and bad behaviour, although that is an unavoidable part of the place. There are some spectacular villa or condo properties to rent or buy, outstanding golf courses, and gorgeous beaches in the northwest well away from the craziness of Patpong. However, if you want beach alternatives, there are other choices close by.

KRABI

Directly across the bay from Phuket, on the western mainland, is Krabi. It is the name of a town, a province, and a slightly more civil way of life. Unlike the usual Thai island resort town that must cater to what tourists want, sex tourism hasn't reached Krabi, and the residents are proud of it. The beaches up and down the coast are pristine, and eighty-three little Robinson Crusoe–like offshore islands are just a short longboat ride away. Krabi has its own international airport just fifteen minutes from the town centre with daily jet service from Singapore, Bangkok, Kuala Lumpur, and Australia.

While there are no beaches in Krabi town proper, just to the south is Ao Nang, a very big beach fronting a tiny town. And yes, there are two very tame girlie bars there but nothing like you would find in Patpong. Hey, this is Thailand. There will always be girls in bars. But there is also a McDonald's and a Starbucks here if that better satisfies your cravings.

From Krabi town or Ao Nang you can take a longboat for a fifteen-minute ride to Railay Beach, a busy spot known for rock climbing and the ultra chic Rayavadee Resort. Just a two-hour boat ride away is Koh Phi Phi island, where Leonardo DiCaprio filmed *The Beach*.

As Krabi gained in expat popularity, it became increasingly evident that the available medical facilities just weren't keeping up. The local hospital is not recommended, and although there are two international hospitals on Phuket Island, it is a two-hour drive to the single bridge on the north shore that connects Phuket to the mainland. In January 2014, the new Krabi Nakharin International Hospital opened for business. It is early days yet to report on the quality of care, but this is a much-needed addition to Krabi and will dramatically increase its appeal as a properly serviced retirement destination for Western retirees.

So you now have a new hospital, a Starbucks, a Tesco with an Apple Store, a McDonald's, and a girlie bar or two. For some people, that's almost perfect.

KOH SAMUI

If you've had enough snow—and what Canadian hasn't?—and beach living is what you want but Phuket is too much action and Krabi is not quite enough, there is another choice. Koh Samui is an island 435 miles (700 kilometres) south of Bangkok in the Gulf of Thailand. It is roughly the same distance from Bangkok as Phuket and Krabi but separated from the Western Andaman Sea and the Indian Ocean by the long narrow Thai mainland. Therefore, no tsunamis here, if that concerns you. Phuket has been hit in the past, and its location makes it a prime target for the next one.

Koh Samui's location in the Gulf of Thailand brings a change in the weather too: April to September here is dry while the rest of the country has its monsoon. Then from October to December it is wet, leaving January to March the hottest, driest months of the year—an ideal recipe for avoiding the worst of a Canadian winter.

Koh is Thai for island, if you haven't figured that out by now. And Koh Samui is true tropical island living. In its favour, it is a very relaxed place, lacking the hustle and all the sex tourism of Phuket but still offering gorgeous beaches and a wide range of accommodation and dining, all with an interesting point of difference to every other beach location in Thailand. The Thai government is actually doing some real positioning here. They want this island to be the calmer, more five-star alternative to the more mass-market, party-hearty destinations (read Phuket).

David

David is British Canadian in his mid-60s. After nearly thirty years of senior corporate positions in Malaysia and Hong Kong, he now runs a small consultancy from Singapore. I have known David for forty years, and I can attest he will never retire. But eight years ago he and his wife bought a beautiful custom-built three-bedroom pool villa for $480,000 in a gated community on the north shore near the airport, in an area called Bangrak.

I asked David about what had attracted him to Thailand. Was it something he had heard or read about? Or something he discovered on his own?

"I lived in Kuala Lumpur, Malaysia, for many years," he said, "but the only Malaysian destination where I would consider buying is Penang. But Penang now is too urban, too busy and built-up to be an island retreat. Thailand offered more options. I bought here versus Phuket as this is smaller—it actually feels like an island, and it isn't the wild and crazy place Phuket has become."

We tend to caution people about some of the perils of buying property, I said. He agreed it isn't the best choice for everyone.

"The purchase of the house was pretty straightforward," he said. "I registered a Malaysian company to buy the property; used myself, my wife, and three local lawyers as the required five directors. I have resignation letters from the lawyers on file should I ever wish to sell."

"I bought here in Koh Samui versus Phuket as this is smaller, it actually feels like an island, and it isn't the crazy place Phuket has become."

In his case and circumstances—and with his experience in Asia—the decision to buy made sense.

"My annual bill for everything to do with the house is just $6,500. That includes electricity, water, security, gardening, house cleaning, and pool maintenance—all in for $550 a month. And I love it. There is a good range of restaurants to suit every taste and budget, from premium Western to local Thai. Eating local is wonderful and very cheap. A Thai restaurant meal of green curry chicken and rice with a beer is less than ten dollars and half that at a food stall. The beaches are excellent, even the hectic Chaweng Beach, which has to be one of the best people-watching beaches in Asia."

David realizes that buying as he did isn't for everyone. And it doesn't need to be a big decision: renting opportunities for the most part are excellent. His advice: keep your options open. That is the whole point of retiring in Southeast Asia.

"I don't think there is any need to buy in Samui unless you want to spend some considerable time here, more than six months a year. Otherwise, there are many villas at every possible price point to rent, short and long term, that won't tie up your money."

Tom

Tom is a Brit in his mid-60s and he has also chosen the north of Koh Samui to build a house with his Thai girlfriend and retire permanently. As a permanent resident, he has a different point of view than David, who spends not much more than a few months a year in residence.

"Unlike other tropical Asian retirement destinations," explained Tom, "Samui runs the gamut from German bricklayers from Munich to beach bums from Sydney to Russian mafia to wealthy Americans. Many at the lower end just exist as they did in their home countries. They have an old scooter, pay low off-beach rents, eat in the noodle shops, drink cheap local beer, and get by on bar and restaurant jobs. You can live very cheaply here, and the point I am making is that this place is not just for the über-rich and not just for the fringe guys; every socio-economic group is represented and that, to me, makes it all the more interesting."

Tom recognizes that Koh Samui's "desert island" status makes it a little more expensive and a bit less accessible than other Thai destinations like Phuket or Bangkok and that suits him. "Yes, it is more expensive here, but it is a nice little island that is relatively unspoiled and much less crowded. In many ways, its isolation is its key benefit."

Tom added, "That extra expense of isolation even carries over to medical care. A comparative minor surgery quote from BNH Hospital Bangkok versus BNH Hospital Koh Samui was 35 per cent more on my little island: same hospital, even the same surgeon! The thing is, they are both fantastic hospitals and, while the cost is higher here, it's still a fraction of costs in the West and the care remains excellent. A reminder—medical insurance—I know some do go without it due to our lower costs but I strongly disagree. It is a must in my opinion."

There is one expense that annoys Tom, David, and every other expat we met.

"The airport is a monopoly run by Bangkok Airways," said Tom. "They set the landing fees for the airlines, which get passed on to customers. Flights in and out to Bangkok, Singapore, and Hong Kong, even with other carriers, are the most expensive in the country. Bloody annoying even if I don't leave the island much anymore."

Exorbitant landing fees aside, Tom has no regrets about his new life on Koh Samui; in fact, he loves it.

"Here in the north, Bangrak has a pleasant beach a few minutes' walk from my house. The little village has a lovely hotel, a variety of really good restaurants, and a supermarket with convenience stores on every block." Getting around is easy as "there are piers for ferries to Koh Phangan and Koh Tao islands and speedboat rentals for anywhere you want to go. The gorgeous Choeng Mon Beach is a five-minute drive away." He says that 75 per cent of the tourists opt for Chaweng and Lamai beaches in the south, and that makes the other beaches the ideal choice for him. "I never go to either one as there are loads of quieter and more charming beaches and villages all over this island."

As appealing as tropical beach life can be, we have found in discussions with friends and travellers we meet that what is alluring about a home can be very different from what attracts us to a beach destination. Going to a beach is a fun holiday, but we don't want to live there. Fair enough. Sand and surf and ocean breezes are not everyone's cup of tea. At least not all the time.

We have talked about the coastal areas of Southern Thailand and the urban charms of Bangkok. It is time we ventured a little further off that well-beaten Thai path.

CHIANG MAI

Chiang Mai is 435 miles (700 kilometres) north of Bangkok and just over 700 years old. The walled city was the capital of the Lanna Kingdom in 1296. The old town is only 1 square mile (2.5 square kilometres) within its ancient walls, and that and its immediate surrounds hold a population of 170,000. More than a million live in its extended market area. There are 20,000 to 30,000 expats, mostly British, American, and Japanese. People feel that the town has largely kept its old charms intact—perhaps one reason is that until the 1920s the only method of reaching Chiang Mai was by elephant.

The weather is a moderate version of Bangkok's seasons due to the city's more northern placement and its higher elevation in the rolling hills leading to the Himalayas. Daytime temperatures are still very warm and very hot in March, April, and May but the nights are cooler than in the south year round. The international airport is well serviced by airlines coming from Bangkok, Singapore, Hong Kong, Taiwan, Korea, Japan, and Mainland China.

We have been to Chiang Mai a few times over the years, and it has the lively feel of the university town that it is. It is bustling with temples, museums, festivals, theatre, sports of all kinds, and a thriving wellness business with many spas and health specialists. I particularly liked the Fish Spa in the busy night market, where hundreds of tiny fish nibble the dead skin off your feet when you dip them in the tank. You can tell by the screams of laughter from the tourists that this is a big draw.

Then there are the elephants. Yes, elephants. You will run into them on the streets, in the parks, just about everywhere. At sanctuaries outside of town, you can have breakfast with them and join them in their morning bath. You might find, though, that feeding an elephant breakfast is sufficient—bathing something that weighs over a ton and moves about is like washing a car stuck in drive.

Dorothy

Dorothy, our 70-year-old English rose, loves the place and claims to be a typical Chiang Mai retiree. We think she is rather more special than typical.

"I could afford to live in the U.K. but I don't want to. My quality of life here is so much better on my pension. I have never, ever doubted my decision to retire in Chiang Mai. I am only anxious, at times, that the Thai government may change the rules concerning expats living here."

Dorothy's story mirrors that of many others in that she had experience in Asia, so picking Thailand was an educated choice. She and her ex-husband were teachers who lived and worked in Singapore for fifteen years. They travelled extensively and their kids became international citizens; her daughter is an academic in the United States and her son is a banker in Singapore.

Dorothy described her life in Chiang Mai as having a pleasant rhythm to it, and it is a healthy one. She is up at six a.m. every morning to hike up the local mountain, Doi Suthep. It is close to her home, so she just rides her scooter there. Remember, Dorothy is 70.

The apartment she owns cost her the equivalent of $85,000. To rent it would be around $500 a month. It is located in the Nimmanhaemin area, just ten minutes' drive from central Chiang Mai. The 1075-square-foot (100-square-metre) one-bedroom apartment is a very modern and comfortable open-plan design. There is a fully equipped gym and a big pool in her complex. As Dorothy said, "It is miles better than my apartment in the U.K. and a quarter of the price."

As for health care, Dorothy takes a sensible approach. "I think it's risky to live here without any health insurance. The company I use will not accept an applicant who is over 60 when you apply." Dorothy's health insurance costs about $3,700 a year. She uses the private clinic at the local public hospital, Sri Pat, and finds the care excellent.

Technology has enabled Dorothy and many other retirees to live comfortably at a distance from family and friends. "I just love Skype," she said. "I can talk to my children whenever I like, and when I call my daughter several times a week our chats can be up to four hours! I can also manage my affairs efficiently on the computer. I have a house in France that I manage on the computer, and I do all my banking on the internet."

In fact, when we met Dorothy, she was selling her house in France, and we found it interesting that between the two, she chose Chiang Mai to retire to.

"Sure, the cheese and wine is cheaper in France but I eat better food here and keep my cholesterol down. There is a better sense of community here than in France or even in the U.K. Older people in Europe don't have as good a quality of life, a healthy, outdoor life. Living here you don't run to the doctor all the time. The climate allows you to exercise year round and stop popping those pills older people take."

"I could afford to retire in the U.K. but I do not want to. My quality of life is so much better here on my pension, and I have never doubted my decision to retire here."

She believes the problems of older people at home are either financial or isolation or both. She said, "I don't have to worry about either of those things here. I have good friends. I am never lonely and never isolated. I can walk around town at all hours in complete safety, much more safe than I would feel at home in the U.K."

Dorothy says her old friends tell her she is "so brave" or "so lucky." She maintains that she is neither. "It is not the least bit hard living here," she stated matter-of-factly. The "lucky" label does annoy her. "You make your own life," she said. "No luck involved."

PROPERTY

Foreigners can legally, and easily, purchase an apartment anywhere in Thailand. However, they cannot own land or houses, at least not outright. However, as we have seen with David in Koh Samui, expats can manage that restriction two ways:

1. Buying the land in the name of a Thai person, usually a friend or someone very trusted, then leasing it back for thirty years with an option to extend. Some developers already offer home or villa sales using their own thirty-year option. While this sounds a bit like Bali's nominee system, in this case it is completely legal.
2. Starting a Thai company in which the foreigner can own up to 49 per cent of the shares and then buy and

own land through the company. In David's case, he used a registered Malaysian company to buy the minority shares, and that is also acceptable.

While these methods are far and away more legally recognized than in Bali, we again think there is a strong case to be made for renting if you want a big villa with a pool and all the trappings. Alternatively, rent or buy a condo apartment where ownership is much more straightforward.

For foreigners to be eligible to purchase an apartment, they must present proof to the Land Department that the funds have been remitted from overseas, in foreign currency. Foreigners can acquire up to, but not exceed, 49 per cent of the floor area of the total building units.

Foreigners can easily and legally
purchase an apartment anywhere in Thailand,
but they cannot own land or houses without
some legal manoeuvring.

COST OF LIVING

Life in Chiang Mai is marginally less expensive than in either Bangkok or Phuket. It is, however, *dramatically* cheaper than in Canada. Groceries are half the cost, and rent is a fraction of what it would be in any Canadian city. So too are restaurants and utilities.

"Electricity is so cheap," said Dorothy almost in embarrassment. Bizarrely, it was initially free for her because she used less than the minimum chargeable amount. That system changed but it is still just a few dollars a month. Water costs Dorothy less

COST OF LIVING

INDICES
Chiang Mai lower than TORONTO

CONSUMER PRICES
49%

RENT
76%

RESTAURANT
71%

GROCERIES
47%

Source: numbeo.com

than $4 a month; high-speed internet service is about $20, and a landline will set you back just over $3. She has house cleaners once a week, two girls for two hours for $10. Getting around in taxis and tuk-tuks is cheap but buying cars, as we have found already in Bali, is not. Dorothy bought a new Honda for $15,000 in 2012 and spent $50 a month on gas. The gasoline bill for her scooter (now traded for the car) is less than $20 a month.

Geoffrey, another Chiang Mai resident, writes books on retiring in Thailand and manages a website to help inform retirees about what's happening around the country.

We met him at a laid-back restaurant on the bank of the Mae Ping River, which meanders through Chiang Mai just fifteen minutes from the old walled town. People sip coffee under trees on an open timber deck and loll away the day listening to the sounds of the river and watching the lush rainforest that rises on the opposite bank. It's rustic and authentic: cane chairs, old wooden tables, and overhead fans whose drowsy rhythms seem to defy time. The food is fantastic too—local Thai—as is the coffee, which is rich and dark. The cost for lunch in this little slice of paradise? Twenty per cent of a similar meal in any Canadian city.

Geoffrey describes Chiang Mai as a carefree but quiet place—very few car horns, ambulances, or police sirens are ever heard. According to him, the major reason expats come to Thailand is financial—but he concedes that most also possess an adventurous spirit. At 73, Geoffrey looks at least ten years younger. He walks for two hours each morning and does yoga three times a week. He relishes his life here, and his apartment is on the river not far from where we are sitting. His monthly living costs are just $900. For this, he gets a rented flat including water and electricity for $300; food costs him another $300 even though he eats out for breakfast, lunch, and dinner every

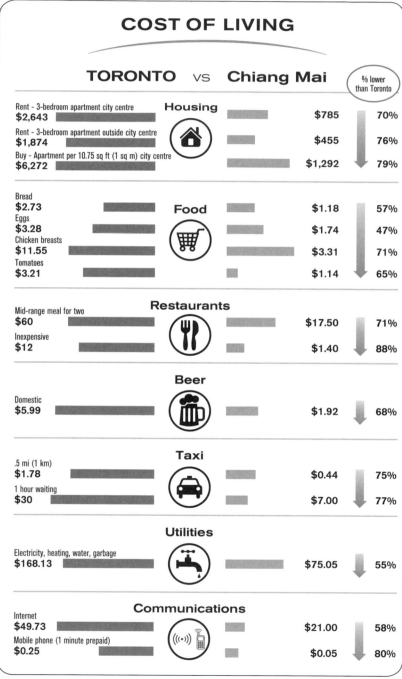

COST OF LIVING

TORONTO vs Chiang Mai

% lower than Toronto

Housing

Item	Toronto	Chiang Mai	% lower
Rent - 3-bedroom apartment city centre	$2,643	$785	70%
Rent - 3-bedroom apartment outside city centre	$1,874	$455	76%
Buy - Apartment per 10.75 sq ft (1 sq m) city centre	$6,272	$1,292	79%

Food

Item	Toronto	Chiang Mai	% lower
Bread	$2.73	$1.18	57%
Eggs	$3.28	$1.74	47%
Chicken breasts	$11.55	$3.31	71%
Tomatoes	$3.21	$1.14	65%

Restaurants

Item	Toronto	Chiang Mai	% lower
Mid-range meal for two	$60	$17.50	71%
Inexpensive	$12	$1.40	88%

Beer

Item	Toronto	Chiang Mai	% lower
Domestic	$5.99	$1.92	68%

Taxi

Item	Toronto	Chiang Mai	% lower
.5 mi (1 km)	$1.78	$0.44	75%
1 hour waiting	$30	$7.00	77%

Utilities

Item	Toronto	Chiang Mai	% lower
Electricity, heating, water, garbage	$168.13	$75.05	55%

Communications

Item	Toronto	Chiang Mai	% lower
Internet	$49.73	$21.00	58%
Mobile phone (1 minute prepaid)	$0.25	$0.05	80%

Source: numbeo.com

day. A new, rented moped costs $120 a month; fuel averages about $30, his internet is $20, and his big extravagance—his yoga classes—are just $90, not a week but a month. Incidentals make up the rest.

A dream-come-true life in Chiang Mai for less than $900 a month. Not bad.

MEDICAL SERVICES

The sophisticated and very reasonably priced medical services in Thailand make it a particularly attractive place for older Canadians to retire to. But it isn't just for retirees—medical and dental tourism is huge in Thailand, with many thousands of Europeans, North Americans, and other Asians coming for treatments of all sorts.

Medical procedures in a large modern hospital, where as many as half the doctors are foreign-trained and the rest are just very good, can cost as little as 10 to 20 per cent of what a procedure would cost in the United States. Charges can be as low as $50 a day for a private room with meals, up to $150 a day for a full suite complete with living room, two bathrooms, a small kitchen, and a bedroom. Patients we spoke to say it is more like staying at a good hotel than a hospital.

These low costs are no excuse not to carry medical insurance if you possibly can. A long-term illness (such as cancer) can still build up a big bill. Then there is the too-common Southeast Asian issue of scooter and motorbike accidents where, for the smallest infraction—such as not having a proper licence or not wearing a helmet—even the insurance you do have will not cover you for the accident.

The good news is that there are dozens of health insurance carriers operating in Thailand, and the premiums are cheaper due to the low cost of high-quality care. Basic premiums as low as $2,000 a year are common, and that is with a reputable London-headquartered firm. Another plus is that medical evacuation insurance is not necessary. The facilities in the country are more than good enough to meet virtually any medical need.

Medical care in a very modern and large hospital, where more than half the doctors are U.S. trained, can cost as little as 10 per cent of what it would cost in the United States.

Ellen and I tested out medical tourism in Bangkok recently. We chose Samitivej Sukhumvit Hospital as it was highly recommended and it represented the upper middle ground of private facilities. The spa-like Bumrungrad International is always in the world's top ten, but you pay more for the swish surroundings. We booked our treatments in advance and found we were assigned a coordinator to escort us to the different departments over two days as it is a very large facility. In the end, we were delighted with the care and the costs. We both had colonoscopies, MRI lung scans, EKGs, and blood work, plus a brief session with a plastic surgeon to laser off all the little facial bumps and lumps that accumulate over the years. The price for both of us was just $2,000 for two full days of treatments.

Medical care is just as good in Chiang Mai, and it is cheaper than Bangkok and in a much more serene location, which, we are told, makes it an ideal choice for medical work that requires a longer-term stay. There are five private hospitals in Chiang Mai, with the Chiangmai Ram Hospital at the top of the list. Even the resort islands are well covered, with both Phuket and Koh Samui served by five or more hospitals on each island.

It is said that Thailand invented medical tourism. They have certainly perfected the model to the point where great care at low cost is a benchmark to aim for in any country, anywhere in the world.

VISAS AND IMMIGRATION

Retirement (referred to officially as Long-Term Stay) visas are readily available in Thailand, and applications can be made within the country or at the Thai embassy in Ottawa or in consulate offices in Toronto, Montreal, Edmonton, and Vancouver.

You must meet one of two financial requirements to obtain a one-year, long-term-stay visa: a lump sum deposit of $27,500 in a Thai bank three months prior to application, or, an income test with the requirement being a minimum of $2,200 a month from pension or other sources. A renewal after the first year requires the financials to remain in place. One additional requirement is to check in with immigration authorities every ninety days but all the expats we spoke to say this is not a problem. A regular tourist visa is not required for visitors from forty-eight countries, including Canadians. However, the visa is valid for only fifteen days.

Tips and Traps: Thailand

1. If you like the hedonistic lifestyle offered by Patpong or Pattaya, good for you. If not, stay away and live in the quieter areas like Chiang Mai or the more upmarket locations like Koh Samui.

➡

2. Thailand offers a vast choice of lifestyles—city Bangkok, beachy and slightly edgy Phuket, the more sophisticated Koh Samui, and the laid-back and slightly bohemian Chiang Mai. There are many more places to choose from, though, such as Mae Sot, a funky little place on the Burmese border or a country retreat spot like Chiang Rai.

3. You are in Buddhist country. Be sensitive to the locals, who are polite and deferential to expats all over the country.

4. Thailand and most of the other Southeast Asian countries offer massive personal freedoms but be aware of the laws of the land. Breaking them can make life very difficult.

5. Choose your neighbourhoods carefully. If it looks seedy and a little dangerous, it is.

6. Thai medical services all over the country are excellent and cheap compared to anything you are familiar with in the West.

7. The cost of living is very low—half of what you would expect at home, and the further you get from tourist areas, the cheaper it gets.

8. Foreigners can buy apartments and condos but not houses or land. You can find legally accepted workarounds, which are much better than the Bali system that attempts to circumnavigate the law.

9. To obtain a Thai visa for a long-term, one-year stay, you must meet clearly stated financial criteria and be prepared to maintain the funds and/or income for a renewal.

FINAL THOUGHT

We love Thailand and have been half a dozen times, visiting all parts of the country. Each visit is a pleasure as there is so much to discover. During the recent coup, we were in Bangkok and had no problem at all. None. While inexpensive, it is more costly than the other destinations we cover. In our search for a new home, it came a very close second.

THE CHECKLIST

1. The cost of living is very low for all things Thai. Western goods, cars, and other purchases not so different than Canada. Thumbs mostly up.
2. Property buying is easy but requires some effort. Apartment and condo buying are very straightforward. Renting is a bargain. Thumbs up.
3. Health care is not only seen as the best in Asia, but is perhaps the best in the world. Big thumbs up.
4. Visas are not hard to obtain and there is a simple immigration process. Even though it is renewable, the long-term stay of one year should be longer to be really good. Thumbs up.

Malaysia

chapter 5

Malaysia:
Paradise Under the Radar

U nlike the more familiar Southeast Asian retirement destinations, such as Bali or Thailand, Malaysia hasn't been at all visible on Canadians' radar. Anybody's radar in fact. We think it's worth thinking about. Have a look, and you will find one of the few undiscovered gems in the region. As a full- or part-time retirement destination, Malaysia truly is a jewel. It has all that expats require and more: a long British colonial history has provided it with English rule of law and English is widely spoken. A now-thriving expat community is centred on Penang Island with all the necessary services and a booming economy with a cost of living that is 50 per cent less than its neighbour, Singapore, to the south. It has a robust medical tourism business rivalling, and in some cases bettering, Thailand.

And Malaysia should be considered for having the most open, sophisticated, and retiree-friendly immigration program in Southeast Asia. It's called MM2H (My Malaysian Second Home) and it is a model for other countries to follow. More on that later.

Malaysia, a former British colony, gained its independence in 1963. Its population of 28 million is made up of 67 per cent Malay, 25 per cent Chinese, and 7 per cent Indian, with all those races practising Islamic, Buddhist, Hindu, and Christian religions.

Imagine all the holidays.

Thanks to how the British chose to divide up Southeast Asia, Malaysia has what could be called a unique geography. There are two zones—East and West—separated by 497 miles (800 kilometres) of the South China Sea. West Malaysia is home to the capital Kuala Lumpur, the dynamic island of Penang, and the vast majority of the population. East Malaysia and its two states of Sabah and Sarawak are on the northern third of the island of Borneo, which is shared with the tiny Kingdom of Brunei and Indonesia. This is the jungle, home to abundant natural resources, nearly impenetrable rainforests, and the impressive Mount Kinabalu. It is the Northwest Territories with palm trees. Why, you may ask, did the British divide Malaysia this way?

Ask them. They did the same thing with East and West Pakistan and stuck a big chunk of India in between.

A better question is why Malaysia is just now being discovered as an expat destination. Andy Davison, CEO of Kuala Lumpur–based The Expat Group, which publishes regional magazines, says that timing—when people have worked in Southeast Asia in past years and when extended families have had country exposure—affects their decision to move there later in their lives. "No one worked here in the 70s and 80s," he said. "Hong Kong and Singapore were the preferred locations for business, banking, shipping, even manufacturing."

According to Andy, these days there are three basic expat groups that have discovered Malaysia. First, there are the people who like the fact that they can spend extended amounts of time here and take advantage of inexpensive property and the tax benefits (no tax on foreign-sourced income). A lot of Japanese, for example, just come here for extended visits. They don't tend to live here year round.

The second group relocates here permanently to take advantage of the low taxes, low cost of property, great weather, and the tropical lifestyle. The largest group for which this is the main attraction are the British and Australians.

A smaller third group comes here to get their kids educated in the excellent school system. Koreans and Japanese dominate this group. Often, the father is still working in Seoul or Tokyo and commutes while mum and the kids have a permanent residence here.

The most popular destinations for foreigners living in Malaysia are Penang Island and its main city, Georgetown, and the country's capital, Kuala Lumpur. About 80 per cent of the total expat population lives in these two centres. Sabah and Sarawak in East Malaysia, due to their remote locations and limited services, have only a few hundred expats.

Although Malaysia is an Islamic country, it is tolerant of other religions and cultures, and the rule of law is firmly rooted in English common law. The constitution of Malaysia allows for a unique dual-justice system—the secular laws (criminal and civil) and Muslim shariah laws. Shariah law applies only to the Islamic community in limited circumstances, and its practice should not put you off the place at all. However, just to add to your peace of mind, there is an island with a progressive government, a robust expat community, a hub for medical tourism, a cost of living that can't be beat, and the local population has a Chinese and Indian majority.

PENANG

Penang Island—off Malaysia's west coast and connected to the mainland by two long bridges—and its state capital, Georgetown (named after King George II), are like a less crowded, greener Hong Kong, and about one-tenth the size. Georgetown is filled to the brim with the legacies of British colonial times: massive government and High Court buildings stretch out behind imposing Greek columns, and enormous Victorian mansions with manicured grounds dot the waterfront in between the giant new condos and shopping malls.

There is another side of compact Georgetown: the Chinese side. It is the marriage of these two sides that earned the city UNESCO World Heritage Site status in 2008. The combination was described as "architecture unparallelled in Asia."

In the central core, surrounded by the grand architectural legacy of the British, are the Chinese Malay shop houses, which were working homes with commercial activity of every description on the ground floor and living quarters above. The upper floors have jalousies, wooden louvred upstairs window shutters, that are often painted bright yellow or turquoise blue, giving these old wood structures a tropical, Caribbean feel.

Now protected by UNESCO, the exteriors can be restored but not altered. However, inside you will find galleries, boutique hotels, chic restaurants, and shops. As a cultural and retail experience, old Georgetown is a joy. However, the city's crushing density tends to lock in the Penang heat and turn off expats from living in the old core. In any case, real estate prices for even a ruin have soared due to the commercial potential.

Think of a tropical version of old Montreal forty years ago when it was just beginning to get gentrified and you can see the potential for what old Georgetown is becoming.

UNESCO designated Georgetown a World Heritage Site in 2008, describing the architecture there as "unparalled in Asia."

Bob

Bob conducted a spreadsheet analysis on the question of where would be the best place in the world to live—that's the kind of guy he is. When it came time for him to retire at age 60, Bob's spreadsheet spat out Penang. It ticked all his boxes for what a guy his age needed to live the good life.

Penang, an island off Malaysia's west coast, which is connected to the mainland by two long bridges, delivered on all Bob's criteria: they included cost of living, health care, crime, climate, and culture.

We had a drink with Bob and his partner, Marion, on the large terrace of their sub-penthouse apartment. The expansive sea views over the Straits of Malacca, north to the mainland, were breathtaking. The apartment is massive, with five bedrooms, five bathrooms, a sauna, a maid's room, and a huge entertaining and kitchen area. The complex has a pool and a fully equipped gym. All this costs 6,500 Ringgit, or just $2,100 a month!

"When you sit around and really start thinking about where you are going to go to retire," Bob said, "it turns out there are a number of criteria that you—everybody really—need to consider. These are taxation, health care, cost of living, crime, climate, and the cultural back story."

His definition of crime is broad and includes not just crime but the justice system, recourse to law, the legal system itself, the corruption of the police, and "even the likelihood of being robbed or kidnapped walking down the street."

Like we said, Bob is über-analytical. In any case, according to Bob, that eliminates a lot of South America and Mexico.

Health care is his next criterion. "There are two issues," he said. "How expensive is it? And how good is it? The United States is expensive. Australia and Singapore are too, but the quality is good. The U.K. is cheap and pretty good. Canada too. Indonesia is just terrible while Thailand and Malaysia are very inexpensive and very good. Here in Southeast Asia, and in particular Malaysia, you don't have the issues with long waits like [you find in] Western countries. Need anything checked or done? It can happen the same day in immaculate facilities by foreign-trained doctors."

As for the cost of living, Bob points out the obvious. If you didn't care about money, you could live anywhere: London, Paris, New York, or the Caribbean. But you will need plenty to live in any of those places. Bob and Marion lived in Switzerland for six months and blew through nearly $90,000 despite having free accommodation with Bob's brother and the use of a car at no cost. Consider their rent now in Penang and how long it would take to burn through ninety grand!

For Bob that was another box ticked for Penang.

Language also ranks high on Bob's decision list. As he says, a dividend of being a former British colony is that English is widely spoken in Malaysia, and even more so in Penang. That gets a big tick. As does Penang's cultural back story.

"Because you speak English," Bob explained, "you know a lot about other English-speaking countries, more than you think. I now know a lot about Canada, the United States, England, and New Zealand from the people we have met, and it is such an easy bond to make. What did I know about Switzerland? Who is their president? What are their laws? How does their odd canton voting system work? When you have no cultural back story and you don't speak the language, it's too tough to live there. I'm sixty, I want my life *to be easy.*"

Bob is the sort of guy who does a spreadsheet analysis on where are the best places in the world to live. When it came time to retire, Bob's spreadsheet spat out Penang.

That, of course, is the bottom line for retiring overseas in Southeast Asia. For instance, do you want it easy or do you want it more adventurous and exotic? We think the joy of Southeast Asia is that you can have one or the other—or just about anything in between—and the price is right. It's all about *what you want.*

Judith

Judith moved to Malaysia in 2007. Her arrival happened a lot faster than she expected. This was due to her MM2H (Malaysia My Second Home) visa being a lot easier to get and being approved a lot more quickly than she thought possible.

She is one of those citizens of the world who has lived in many places. Born in the United Kingdom, she left at 21 and lived in South America, South Africa, Australia, and Spain. She never even considered returning to the U.K. as she approached retirement age. "I hate it," she said. "Can't stand the place, the people, the weather, their conservative nature. I would rather be in Australia if I could afford it. I think I should have been born there."

Of her Malaysian decision, she explained, "I had heard about their visa program. I just e-mailed the Malay government and said I fancied becoming a resident and getting an MM2H visa. What do I have to do?"

She said they e-mailed her right back with a list of documents they would need to process a visa: a copy of her passport, details of her income, and proof of medical insurance. These had to be certified by a notary. When she sent them off, she admitted she expected the processing period would take months. To her surprise—her shock—she received her visa in only a few weeks! She had six months to activate her new visa.

"Well, I panicked," she said, laughing at the memory. "I needed to get over to Malaysia, put money in a bank account, have a medical, and then the visa was instant. It took me less than seven days to make it all happen."

But then Judith was faced with another problem: where to live.

"It had been years since I had been to Malaysia," she said. "I didn't know where to live. I started looking in Kuala Lumpur, downtown, in the suburbs and just talked to people."

Judith had struck me as a woman of remarkable confidence, but what she said surprised me.

"I'm a country girl at heart," she said, and admitted that at first "it was daunting, really." A group of Norwegian friends were living on the top floor of a complex in Times Square, right in the centre of downtown. "But it was so busy." Not her thing at all. Judith was more down-home prairie than downtown Toronto or Vancouver.

So she gave up on Kuala Lumpur. She rented a car and drove all over Malaysia. She was keen on the island of Langkawi, about 75 miles (120 kilometres) north of Penang. She spoke to residents there and knew it was going to be a solitary and isolated life on a small island. It would take about three hours to get to Penang by boat or a couple of hours by car.

"It is lovely," Judith said. "It is a tourist island with gorgeous beaches. Here in Penang the beaches are not so good." Langkawi turned out to be a great place to visit, but she realized that living there would be difficult. If she got sick, she would have to come all the way up to Penang, and that just wasn't going to work.

Judith finished her search by deciding on Penang, where she has been renting property since 2010. She wisely took her time to settle in. "Once I had my visa, I was in no hurry. I visited often but I sorted myself out first. I find it very busy in Penang, but it is growing on me. I'm not sure if I will spend the rest of my life here—the traffic drives me crazy—but I am liking it more and more because it is just so interesting. There are a huge number of cultures and religions here."

She added, "I like the people. The food is great. There is lots to do. I joined the International Women's Association. It's a great way to meet people as I'm not all that gregarious and it's not easy for a single person. They have everything from organized card games to film nights to dinners that helped me get and stay engaged."

Bob, our spreadsheet guy, provided me—not surprisingly— with a detailed perspective of the Penang expat factor.

"You are living on an island of about 700,000 people but it is more like living in a village with a much smaller population. I have done the math two or three different ways, and I get to the same number each time. I work out that there are 2,000 to 3,000 expats on Penang. That community is incredibly well connected."

It sounds very agreeable. Almost ideal. Bob agreed but then demurred, as if professionally obliged to be objective.

"If there is a downside to it," he admitted, "it is that all 3,000 expats go to the same shopping malls, the same dry cleaner, the same bars and restaurants."

But for Bob the numbers don't lie, and what the numbers tell him is all good. He loves being part of a rich and diverse community of expats. For instance, he said, without too much effort, "by tomorrow night we could have a dinner party with the following demographics: a professional chef (or two), a woman who runs a modelling agency, an orchestra conductor, several professors, some senior military guys, a security expert, a chaplain, even a jockey." He smiled broadly. "We are swimming in an incredibly rich social pool here, much deeper than we ever had at home." He gave me a "think about it" look. "And for me, that is the biggest advantage over places like Thailand. Now maybe I'm being a snob—I just don't think a sex tourist would be as charming a dinner companion, and there are way too many of them in Thailand."

The majority of expats in Malaysia live, as Bob and Marion do, overlooking the breezy waterfront along Gurney Drive just outside of Georgetown proper and the old town that lies within. Here you find a dozen stylish condos off the promenade and two spanking-new shopping malls. The condo units are enormous in most instances, some up to and over 10,000 square feet (930 square metres)! Four to five thousand square feet (370 to 465 square metres) is common. Even for these vast spaces, rents for a fully furnished 5,000-square-foot unit are hardly ever more than $3,000 a month, and that is for the biggest, highest floor units.

Surprisingly, the cost to buy is not nearly as cheap—this is a very concentrated and preferred area of offshore property for investors and speculators from Singapore and China. When you consider the return on investment on a $3-million apartment renting for just over $2,000 a month, it makes renting look very, very smart. Also in its favour, it is just a few minutes' walk into old town and all its restaurants, coffee shops, galleries, and stores.

To the north of Gurney Drive is the new development of Quayside. Hundreds of condo units and townhouses are all placed close by the central waterfront mall, which contains a hotel and retail and gourmet shops as well as a marina. Again, it is expensive to buy here (although not as pricey as Gurney Drive) but extraordinarily inexpensive to rent. Condos and apartments are smaller, in the 2,500-square-foot (230-square-metre) range, and go for $2,000 a month, or less. Still further to the north is the community of Batu Ferringhi, the most developed beach area on the island and home to over a dozen hotels catering to every budget. There is a lively night market and many condos and townhouse properties to choose from. Although the beaches here are big and appealing from a distance, on closer viewing the water is far from clean due to years of poorly regulated development, and there is the occasional invasion of jellyfish to contend with. Nothing like a dirty, stinging jellyfish to keep you out of the water.

As for the entire west side of the island, it is pristine. No development, no condos, no malls. It is all protected nature reserve.

Penang, and indeed a lot of Malaysia,
is relatively Western compared to Vietnam or
Cambodia. Expats call it "Asia light."

The renewal of old Georgetown is moving at a blistering pace. Two hotel entrepreneurs, Christopher Ong and Karl Steinberg—well known in Asia for their (now-sold) Galle Fort Hotel in Sri Lanka—have developed a number of restaurants and boutique hotels in the old town. They began with Muntri Mews; once an old stable for rickshaws, carriages, and carts, it is now a budget hotel with a small café tucked into a wonderful tropical garden. Next they opened Noordin Mews, an upscale version of their first property, with a pool off the equally lovely garden.

Recently, they returned to their five-star heritage with the Seven Terraces, a luxurious and romantic eighteen-suite boutique hotel created out of seven abandoned shop houses, with a gorgeous restaurant and antique furniture store. Another fantastic property, by Narelle McMurtrie, is ChinaHouse. It is a 400-foot-long, 25-foot-wide (122-metre by 7.5-metre) shop house with an espresso bar, a bakery, a wine store, bistro dining, a formal dining room, and a courtyard burger bar that doubles as a jazz club on weekends. On the second floor is a wonderful gallery, pop-up retail space, and a reading room. We have headed to ChinaHouse in the mid-afternoon for a gallery show, had dinner, and then gone to the jazz bar where we stayed until after midnight. A one-stop entertainment centre.

KUALA LUMPUR

Another option for expats is the country's capital, Kuala Lumpur (or just KL) as everyone calls it. It is not an old city; it was formed in 1850 when tin was first mined from the two rivers that run through town. A decade later, the two opposing warlords who controlled tin production spent more time fighting each other than mining tin. That prompted the British to come in, settle the issue, and appoint a Chinese headman to run the town.

In 1881 a series of devastating fires that shut down tin production prompted the British once again to intervene and require that all buildings be constructed of fireproof brick and tile. Think what you might about the Brits and their colonial methods, but it is doubtful that places like KL would even exist today without them. Modern KL has a population of 2 million people, and 7 million live in the extended market area. Recently recognized for the striking Petronas Twin Towers, hosting the 1998 Commonwealth Games, and now the Formula One World Championship in nearby Sepang, KL is the political, economic, and cultural hub of the nation. That said, while it has none of the sleaziness of Bangkok, neither is it as cutting edge socially or culturally. Nor is it as international as Bangkok or as important as Singapore as a trading and commercial centre.

But it is an easy, affordable, and comfortable place compared to most other Southeast Asian cities.

The infrastructure here (roads, power, etc.) is first world, as it is in most of Malaysia. It is a picture of calm and Western-like orderliness compared to Jakarta, Saigon, or Bangkok. The medical facilities are top-notch and include the Prince Court Medical Centre, judged to be the best medical tourism hospital in the world. KL is also a great base for low-cost travel around the region. The discount airline AirAsia is based here with its own new terminal that opened in 2014. The place has its good points. The shopping is good, and the bars and restaurants around Bukit Bintang get a good buzz going on Friday and Saturday nights. And, as always in Malaysia, the food is superb with an extraordinary choice of restaurants.

Unlike Chinese-dominated Penang, KL is the Muslim power base of the country. Ostensibly, the country is a proper democracy but a tightly controlled one with the media under close government supervision and a compliant judiciary keeping opposition parties in check. Although there is still the British legacy of values and the remnants of English culture, we would suggest KL needs to loosen up for it to be a top-tier expat retirement destination.

> Malaysia is a very comfortable place for retirees to live. Yes, it is an Islamic country. But it is tolerant of other religions and cultures, and secular law is based on English common law.

IPOH

The town of Ipoh was the centre of the tin-mining business in the Kinta Valley at the turn of the twentieth century. It nestles between the Cameron Highlands with its tea plantations and old British resorts and the coast, less than three hours' drive north of Kuala Lumpur. Many great fortunes were made here, and the grand colonial architecture reflects the town's importance in a bygone industrial age.

Today, the town has a population of just over 200,000. Leafy poincianas hang across the main road as you enter from KL off the excellent North–South Expressway. The Kinta River winds through town, with bars and restaurants lining its banks. Rising above Ipoh are the misty mountains of the Cameron Highlands 56 miles (90 kilometres) away. We watch a thunderstorm march down the valley, leaving behind a massive rainbow gleaming in the sun. Dorothy, we are not in Kansas anymore.

Jack and Olga

We sat on a covered apartment terrace one afternoon looking toward the Cameron Highlands and watching the storm roll down the valley. The temperature cooled, and the hot and fragrant local tea braced us for the cool breezes to follow.

The apartment is owned by Jack and Olga, who visit Ipoh regularly from their native Australia. Jack, a principal of an engineering company, lived in Ipoh when tin was still being mined in the early 1970s and fell in love with the place. He tells how friends would gather in his upstairs sitting room in the evenings to drink cold beers under the swirling ceiling fans. The occasional bat or two would join them, causing them to open the shutters wide and crank up the fans to get rid of them.

Jack and Olga bought their three-bedroom, three-bathroom apartment for about $95,000 a dozen years ago. This is not a town for property speculators, so it isn't worth much more than that today. They spend several months a year here, and if economics forced a decision between Australia and Ipoh, it would be Ipoh they would call home.

And why not? The town has touches of old Malaysia. It has a rich green patina with gorgeous tall trees and enormous leafy plants. Ipoh also offers an inexpensive cost of living and food to die for. Ipoh is famous within Malaysia for its food and even more so for its amazing coffee, which is grown on the slopes of the Cameron Highlands. Coffee houses dot the town, but they have nothing in common with the prefabricated corporate-run one-size-fits-all outlets we are familiar with in Canada. In short, put down your mass-produced doughnut and that "cappuccino" that tastes more like tepid dishwater and prepare to be dazzled. Coffee houses here are traditional Asian-style eating areas, often open air, with central seating surrounded by a wondrous array of food stalls. You wander about choosing from satays, noodles, curries, and grilled fish and chicken prepared in the unique Ipoh style. It is exotic, delicious, and cheap, and each dish is just over $1. A cold beer is expensive at $2.

There are few Westerners in Ipoh. It is primarily a Chinese town—and some mega-rich Chinese Malays live here. One of the town's residents is the owner of a giant global property development group and another owns the global cosmetics retailer Crabtree & Evelyn. While Ipoh today may seem a little out of the mainstream, the tin-mine owners' presence has always made it a rather grand and wealthy town. Many of the locals sent their children to Oxford and Cambridge and followed British colonial traditions. As they prospered, they began keeping leafy estates far off in England or Australia. The old money is still very much here, just a little faded over time.

Standing out among the reflections of Ipoh's colonial past is the 120-year-old, sprawling, white-walled Royal Ipoh Club. With spacious verandas and frangipani-filled gardens, it is a snapshot of the town's patrician history. Today, sipping an afternoon gin and tonic on the veranda, you can imagine watching a cricket match a hundred years ago with players in their crisp regulation whites silhouetted against the lush green pitch. Once, this was the exclusive bastion of elite British wealth and snobbery; no other races allowed. Today, it is easy for anyone to become a member, and the board of directors, once all white and English, are now all Indian Malays.

Ipoh also serves as the gateway to the Cameron Highlands. Singapore Airlines has direct flights into Ipoh, testimony to the appeal of the hilltop retreat built by the British in the 1930s. The Brits developed the area because its higher elevation, up to 6,560 feet (2,000 metres), provided a much cooler climate than the lowlands near the coast. Here, the temperature year round never rises above 77 degrees Fahrenheit (25 degrees Celsius) in the daytime. The cooler weather also supports tea, coffee, and strawberry plantations, and, as the British must always have, a golf course. That original six-hole course is a full eighteen today and attached to the wonderful Cameron Highlands Resort.

Ipoh and surrounding area has a lot to offer for the more adventurous type. It is very foreigner friendly but you won't find a large Western community here. Not yet anyway. There are new condo and apartment buildings, configured much like Jack's place, in which you can rent a spacious three-bedroom, two-and-a-half bathroom, with a view to the Highlands, for just $450 a month. And you can buy it for less than $100,000. We predict that, in not too many years, the elegant surroundings and ultra-cheap cost of living could make this a key retirement destination.

JOHOR

We would be remiss if we didn't mention Johor as a possible destination for retiring Canadians. Situated at the very southern tip of Malaysia, it is right across the causeway from the island of Singapore. For the past fifteen years, as the cost of living in slick Singapore has soared, Johor has increasingly become a bedroom community for its larger neighbour. It's only thirty or forty minutes from Singapore's central financial district via the causeway, or another new bridge to the west creatively named the Second Link, but prices for groceries, gasoline, cars, and other goods here are a fraction of Singapore's. Some people love it, some not so much.

As well as dozens of old and new condos, there are also estate properties like Horizon Hills and Leisure Farm Resort. In our view, *estate* is a gentrified naming alternative to a secure gated property.

While Johor was once just a cheap housing option, now it is trying to move upscale. But it hasn't yet left behind its reputation for being a second-tier, slightly remote outpost in a high-crime area. There have been home invasions, purse snatchings, and car jackings—all things that terrify Singaporeans and lead them to perpetuate the stories and, no doubt, embellish them on occasion. To be fair, Johor has had its share of security issues in the past. What it will become in the future is the question.

We've been there many times (there are excellent golf courses on those protected estates), and it never seemed as bad as it is made out to be. Still, that was just a golf game, in daylight. It takes less than ninety minutes from downtown Singapore to be on the first tee of a lovely golf course. We do find it hard to recommend a place with no real core or culture (other than golf) and no real reason to be other than a low-cost alternative to its rich neighbour.

Clearly, an inexpensive gated life appeals to some people even if it isn't high on our personal list as a retirement destination.

PROPERTY: RENTING

A tremendous amount of development is taking place in the key expat areas of Malaysia. In other country chapters, we have strongly suggested renting before you buy to ensure the place is right for you and, in some instances, to avoid complicated issues associated with purchasing.

COST OF LIVING

INDICES

Penang lower than **TORONTO**

CONSUMER PRICES
45%

RENT
77%

RESTAURANT
62%

GROCERIES
47%

Source: numbeo.com

Malaysia has a unique situation in which rents are impossibly low in relation to purchase prices. Look at Bob and Marion's deal in Penang. They are renting a massive and luxurious five-bedroom apartment on Gurney Drive overlooking the water for $2,100 a month. To buy that same apartment would be over $2 million. Do the math: the ROI for a property investor is terrible. For the renter, it is fabulous.

Of course, even that monthly rent may be more than a retiree wants to pay, and it certainly may be much more space than they would ever need. Bob and Marion's place is clearly at the five-star end of the scale. For people of more modest means and needs, the news is even better.

Rent in Kuala Lumpur for a comfortable, furnished two-bedroom, two-bathroom apartment starts from $150 a week. It goes up from there—a luxury apartment downtown with a pool, gym, and parking costs about $1,800 a month.

In Penang, a large three-bedroom furnished apartment, such as Gurney Park, virtually on the water and a walk to old Georgetown, rents for less than $1,000 a month.

And in Ipoh, like Jack and Olga, you can rent a spacious three-bedroom looking up at the Cameron Highlands for $450 a month or buy it for $100,000 or less.

PROPERTY: BUYING

Non-residents are allowed to purchase residential and commercial property outright in Malaysia, although with some restrictions. The property laws are based on the Australian system whereby the rights of foreigners to own and possess property, and to seek legal redress in the courts, are guaranteed in law.

All purchasers are subject to restrictions on Malay reserved lands and restricted from buying properties allocated for ethnic

Malays (known as *Bumiputras*, they get special considerations over all other races). The minimum investment is $170,000 for foreigners but this amount varies by state. In Penang, for example, the state government has raised the floor price of property for foreign buyers to $340,000 in their efforts to seek a better class of buyer. Landed property has a $700,000 purchase minimum. Below is a description of the four kinds of titles that apply in Malaysia. Although the term "Malay Reserved Land" rarely comes up for expats, it is an added twist. One of the reasons the beautiful island of Langkawi is relatively undeveloped is that much of the better land, beachfront in particular, is reserved for Malays only.

OWNERSHIP TITLES

Freehold Freehold property belongs to the owner in perpetuity. Transfer of interest in the property can proceed without any restrictions or approvals from the government.

Leasehold Land leased by the government for a specific term, most commonly in the duration of 33 years or 99 years. The land will automatically return to the State Authority upon the expiry of the leasehold term. Transfer of interest to another party may require State Authority approval.

Landed Issued for properties built on individual plots of land that is subdivided horizontally.

Strata A form of ownership commonly found within residential and commercial multi-storey buildings, as well as landed properties within a gated community. Strata title properties comprise individual lots owned by individual owners and common property, which is defined as everything else on the parcel of land, such as the common stairwell, driveways, roof, etc.

Malay Reserve Land Article 89 of the Malaysian Constitution states that a person of the Malay ethnicity may own
land or possess an interest in a Malay Reservation Area.
A Malay Holding includes any alienated land within a
Malay Reservation Area that has been duly declared and
gazetted as a registered interest of a Malay citizen, a pro-
prietor, or co-proprietor. Once land is gazetted as a Malay
Reservation Area, it can only be sold, leased, or otherwise
disposed of only to Malay individuals or corporations.

From 2010, the effective capital gains tax rate of selling
a property has been set at 5 per cent. No tax is imposed on
profits after five or more years of ownership. However, always
check for changes in tax laws before you buy. The national
bank, Bank Negara Malaysia, does not impose any restrictions
on repatriation of profits on property or even proceeds from
the divestment of investments in Malaysia. Income earned in
the country will be taxed. (See chapter 8.)

COST OF LIVING

Penang, Kuala Lumpur, Ipoh, and perhaps Johor are all excellent low-cost options for a retiring Canadian.

Grant, a middle-aged early retiree, said, "Here in Penang it
is easy Asia. About 99 per cent of the people in Penang speak
English, it is inexpensive, laid-back, and relaxed." While not
dirt cheap like the less developed countries of Southeast Asia,
it is a lot cheaper than Canada.

Renting a three-bedroom apartment in a very nice waterfront area of Penang or in downtown KL can be 60 to 70 per
cent less than a Toronto equivalent. Good internet access is
available from four or five providers for $50 a month, unlimited

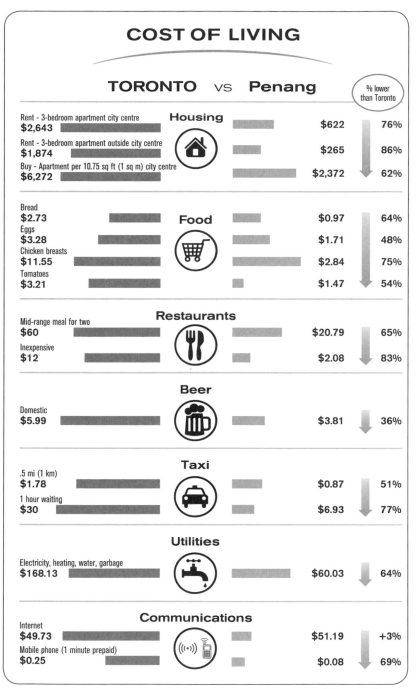

COST OF LIVING

TORONTO vs Penang

% lower than Toronto

Housing

	Toronto	Penang	% lower
Rent - 3-bedroom apartment city centre	$2,643	$622	76%
Rent - 3-bedroom apartment outside city centre	$1,874	$265	86%
Buy - Apartment per 10.75 sq ft (1 sq m) city centre	$6,272	$2,372	62%

Food

	Toronto	Penang	% lower
Bread	$2.73	$0.97	64%
Eggs	$3.28	$1.71	48%
Chicken breasts	$11.55	$2.84	75%
Tomatoes	$3.21	$1.47	54%

Restaurants

	Toronto	Penang	% lower
Mid-range meal for two	$60	$20.79	65%
Inexpensive	$12	$2.08	83%

Beer

	Toronto	Penang	% lower
Domestic	$5.99	$3.81	36%

Taxi

	Toronto	Penang	% lower
.5 mi (1 km)	$1.78	$0.87	51%
1 hour waiting	$30	$6.93	77%

Utilities

	Toronto	Penang	% lower
Electricity, heating, water, garbage	$168.13	$60.03	64%

Communications

	Toronto	Penang	% lower
Internet	$49.73	$51.19	+3%
Mobile phone (1 minute prepaid)	$0.25	$0.08	69%

Source: numbeo.com

downloads. A cellphone on contract is $18 a month. A land-line, free with an internet contract, includes a handset.

A three-course meal in a nice restaurant is 70 per cent less than at home. I can vouch for this myself. Recently, in Penang's lovely Pulau Tikus market I had fried egg noodles (called *mee*) with bean sprouts, green onions, chicken, coriander, and chilies for 86 cents. A big cup of strong coffee was 50 cents. Groceries are 30 to 40 per cent less, or even more if you shop the markets and not the Western grocery stores. Grant added, "We shop at what they call the wet market (not really wet, just local) once a week. There is no bargaining, it is a set price—not a foreigner price—we pay the same as the locals do." Grant reckons fruit and vegetables for the week cost him less than $20 for a family of four. He gets fresh chicken and fish—"and by that I mean a gorgeous plump white-skinned chicken that was alive fifteen minutes ago"—for a fraction of the cost to a Canadian. "We buy chicken breasts to feed our gang of four for less than a dollar each."

For Grant and his wife, Fiona, the decision to move to Malaysia was as much about lifestyle as it was about an inexpensive cost of living. They found both. Both keen divers, they regularly dive off the coast of Langkawi but also drive to the Perhentian Islands off the east coast, a six-hour drive from Penang. "It is the most glorious place. The water is a transparent blue, and the island's accommodations are so incredibly cheap. We rent a shack right on the beach, put hammocks up between the palm trees, and just relax," Fiona said.

Not everything is inexpensive. Although a water bill is just $2 a month, electricity costs can be high because air conditioning giant condo spaces in a tropical climate can be costly. Expect a monthly bill of $250 or higher if your space is in the 4,000- to 5,000-square-foot (370- to 465-square-metre) range. Cars are heavily taxed, especially imported cars. Locally produced vehicles such as Protons and Peroduas are cheap as chips but tend to have the build quality of the Ladas we used to buy in Canada in the 70s. But of course, no rust problems here. Expect to pay $20,000 for a locally produced seven-passenger people mover.

MEDICAL SERVICES

One of the great attractions of Malaysia for a retiree is the country's excellent medical services and facilities. Like Thailand, Malaysia is a prime destination for medical tourism. There are seventy flights a week from Indonesia to Penang alone, made up of Indonesians seeking quality medical care. The Prince Court Medical Centre in Kuala Lumpur is ranked number one in the world for medical tourism—better than Bangkok, better than Singapore, better than North America, and better than Europe.

In Penang, we met up with Kendall and her family, and they have no medical insurance.

"We cancelled it," she said.

That seemed very risky. She explained her decision.

"Most expats don't worry much about insurance unless the company they work for pays for it. The medical care here is very good, with nearly 100 per cent of medical staff internationally qualified. The dentists too are excellent and cheap. You can walk right in to a GP, no appointment required. For us, an appointment, consultation, and antibiotics cost $25. Pharmacists here sell everything you need over the counter." There are nine hospitals on the island of Penang, she said, at least half of which service the international medical tourism business. "I have heard no horror stories here about quality of care. Just simply excellent."

Kendall is under 55, and having medical insurance isn't an issue for her ... yet. But Ellen, who lives in Kuala Lumpur, is 67 and she doesn't have it either. To the average risk-averse Canadian—like me—that decision seemed beyond risky. Ellen explained that people over 65 have a hard time getting insurance coverage if they didn't sign up when they were younger. But, according to her, the standard of services in KL is so good and the costs so reasonable that she is not worried.

> One of the great attractions of Malaysia
> for those over 55 years of age is the country's
> excellent medical services and facilities.
> They are on par with Thailand and compete
> with the Thais' for medical tourism.

Medical treatments that may cost hundreds of thousands of dollars in Singapore or Sydney without health coverage, she points out, would cost only a few tens of thousands in Malaysia. "I take that into account. I know that I need to set aside enough money to cover a big medical bill if I got really ill."

We admit that such an approach—such an attitude—may be difficult to accept. Frankly, we have a hard time with it. But what you know is what you are used to, right? Just because we proudly live in Canada and tout our universal health care to the Americans doesn't mean our health care system functions as well as the better Asian ones.

Despite high-quality and inexpensive care, as we have suggested for other low-cost countries, if you can possibly get medical insurance, get it. If you are a part-time resident keeping your Canadian coverage, supplement it with a reasonable travel insurance policy that provides medical evacuation. At least check your province's services because what they provide offshore can vary. (See chapter 9.)

VISAS AND IMMIGRATION

Malaysia is the most retiree-friendly country in Southeast Asia. The MM2H (Malaysia My Second Home) program offers foreigners a renewable, ten-year, multiple-entry visa. It gives certainty of tenure, it's a streamlined application process, and it's tax friendly. All non-Malaysian–sourced income, including pensions, is tax-free to MM2H visa holders.

Different requirements are in place for applicants under 50 years of age and for those over 50. If you're under 50, you will need proof of liquid assets of $170,000 and a demonstrated monthly income of $3,400.

For applicants over 50, the requirement drops to proof of assets of $118,000, a fixed deposit of $50,000, and the same level of monthly income as for under-50s. The fixed deposit earns interest and that interest is tax-free.

That fixed deposit can be reduced if you buy property in Malaysia, if you have medical expenses that are deductible, or if you deduct payments for children's education, which you are allowed to do. Although you are required to have medical insurance, the authorities will immediately waive that if you are turned down on the basis of age. A clean home-country police report and an in-country medical checkup are also required. Once your visa is granted, you have six months to activate it.

The visa allows you to bring in parents over age 60 on a one-year renewable visa and covers your children up to age 21 as dependants. It allows you to buy a locally produced car tax-free or to import a car tax- and duty-free.

> *The MM2H visa is unique in the world as it is the only visa designed to attract retirees with a list of benefits that no other country, Western or Asian, currently provides.*

This is a very good deal. However, in the event you don't have that kind of money to invest, a normal tourist visa for entering Malaysia is good for ninety days (not three months, ninety days) and can be renewed every time you leave the country. Unlike other countries (such as Singapore), a simple standard visa allows you to rent a condo, get a cellphone, sign up for utilities, etc. You do need the visa to get a Malay driver's licence or to purchase a car. (See chapter 10.)

Tips and Traps: Malaysia

1. Health care in Malaysia, like Thailand, is cheap and of very high quality. You can confidently use the medical system in Penang and Kuala Lumpur as it is ranked among the very best in the world. Medical insurance is not a must-have here, but good to have.

2. Malaysia is marketing itself to foreigners and that includes retirees. The requirements are not onerous but proof of assets and different fixed deposit levels for people over or under 50 are required. The East Malaysia states of Sabah and Sarawak require

separate applications made directly to their state governments.

3. Malaysians are super friendly and quite Eurocentric. A long colonial history and an orderly independence in 1957 have left a legacy of good feelings for foreigners.

4. Malaysia is Asia-easy. But don't be naïve. Expats are certainly more wealthy than most of the locals. Be sensible. Don't make yourself a target for petty crime.

5. Malaysia is a Muslim country. But it is moderate Muslim, particularly in Penang, which is dominated politically and economically by Malay Chinese.

6. There are many places for Canadian retirees to settle, such as Ipoh, Langkawi, Penang, KL, or Johor. The excellent road system makes it easy to drive all over the country. Each destination has its merits.

7. Rents are significantly cheaper than at home—as much as 70 per cent less. Buying property is comparatively easy compared to other countries but prices in preferred areas can be unreasonably high. Renting here is the best option, by far.

8. The cost of living is very inexpensive but still more than the less developed countries in Southeast Asia such as Vietnam and Cambodia. In Penang and KL you do get the Western services expats and retirees tend to require, and we think that is worth the small premium you pay.

FINAL THOUGHT

Malaysia has been a bit of an enigma as it fell off, or really never made, the expat radar for decades. Now, it is a premier choice for expat retirees as an affordable, friendly, safe, and sophisticated destination. It is not scrubbed and sanitized like Singapore, nor is it sexy–crazy like parts of Thailand. It has some edge and a little third world to it, but it is first world all the way in all the things that matter to a Canadian retiree.

THE CHECKLIST

1. The cost of living is extremely low. Western goods are not bad overall, and local cars are highly taxed but cheap. Thumbs up.
2. Foreigners can buy property and hold title. No issues. Some minimums apply on price. Renting is an absolute bargain. Thumbs up.
3. Health care in Penang and Kuala Lumpur is excellent, as good as or better than Thailand. Thumbs up.
4. Visas are no fuss whatsoever for standard ninety-day tourism entry. The sophisticated MM2H program is unrivalled in all of Asia and, frankly, a model for any country, anywhere. Thumbs up.

chapter 6

Vietnam:
A Country in Transition

Vietnam is a country steeped in the contrasting aromas of sharp spices and sweet flowers. It's an ancient culture with a long and fascinating history. Unfortunately, for most outsiders, in more recent times it is seen as the wrong kind of history.

The reality of modern Vietnam might come as a shock—a very pleasant shock. Today, it is one of the most friendly and vibrant countries in all of Southeast Asia. For Canadians pondering a retirement destination a step or two off the beaten path, it may be one of the best—and least publicized—bargains that exists. The economy is stable, the government is progressive, the people are delightful, and the food, well, the food is simply wonderful (we have had unforgettable meals that cost literally no more than the change I had in my pocket at the time).

It wasn't always like this.

Vietnam

Thirty years ago, Vietnam was still clawing its way back to some kind of normalcy after five decades of war with the Japanese, the French, and, finally, the Americans. Having beaten back every invader, the country faced some of the bleakest years in its history from 1975 to 1986.

Brilliant, relentless, and unconquerable at war, they couldn't manage peace.

There was no post-war economic plan, no business structure, no private enterprise, and the typical communist state-led economy of collective agricultural and industrial five-year plans was an abject failure.

But then they had a big idea: a top-down process of reform. And it worked.

The government saw an opportunity to develop a socialist-oriented market economy where the state would play a decisive role in directing the economy, but private enterprise and co-operatives would play a significant role in commodity production. Socialism replaced communism.

They called it *doi moi* (reform). In 1986 the policy was implemented. It was quickly followed by an ambitious succession of reforms to land law, tax law, bankruptcy law, and environmental law; a labour code; and dozens more initiatives designed to accelerate the country from a state-led, peasant-driven centrist system to a market economy.

They went from a feudal system to a modern one with the stroke of a pen. I suspect it wasn't as easy as that.

Nearly three decades on, Vietnam has transformed itself in ways few could have imagined. In the early 90s the World Bank estimated the national poverty rate of Vietnam to be roughly 60 per cent of the population at or below the poverty line. In 2012 that same figure had shrunk to just 17 per cent. It has fallen to high single digits today.

The economy has improved, but not for everyone; there are still serious income gaps. However, overall, Vietnam's dramatic rise from one of the world's poorest nations to a middle-income country is nothing short of remarkable.

The average life expectancy was barely 50 in the 1960s (a few decades of war can do that) but has climbed to over 75 years today. The country has abundant natural resources and a large and inexpensive work force that is keen to participate in the economic miracle. Foreign trade was less than US$500 million before *doi moi*; today it is nearly US$40 *billion*. From selling goods to fewer than 40, mostly communist, governments in 1990, it now sells to 167 countries and has trade agreements with over 80.

Things have changed, almost all for the better.

> *The implementation of doi moi, or reform, in 1986 opened the country to both economic growth and improvements to quality of life on a scale never seen before in a communist country.*

It has been widely documented that Vietnam's dramatic growth has slowed in the last few years. Economic expansion at around 5 per cent is on par with most developing nations but below its booming Southeast Asian neighbours. The inevitable Asian income gap between the nation's highest and lowest earners has appeared, just as it has in the other Southeast Asian countries. The middle and lower classes, after making great gains, may have reached the limit of their opportunity. It could take the next generation, better educated (half the country's young population now are university graduates), to jump-start a return to a robust middle-class growth curve a few years from now.

With nearly ten years of growth at about 20 per cent a year, perhaps they needed the break to catch up.

On a scale from developing to developed, a Canadian retiree probably will find that Vietnam is in the positively developing category; it is not yet a Malaysia or a Thailand but is gaining ground quickly. Although it is one of the most engaging countries in Southeast Asia, and drop-dead gorgeous from the north to the south, it lacks the modern infrastructure, systems, and organization of its more developed neighbours. Just spend some time in the endless line-up for a visa on arrival at Da Nang airport, and you will experience near comical bureaucracy to a degree you would never think possible. The system is completely manual, requiring you to fill out a form, hand it in at a window with your passport, wait in a mosh pit with dozens of others until it is your passport being waved about, and then pay cash, but only in American dollars.

This is going to take some time to fix.

THE VIETNAM WAR

It is difficult to write about Vietnam or, indeed, visit the country without touching on war (the French War or the more recent American War, as the locals call them). The memorials and the museums are ubiquitous throughout the country's cities and towns, created in large part by the incredible amounts of war materiels the United States left behind. Our impression is that the Vietnamese are working very hard to put the past behind them, to move on and join ranks with the rest of the modern world, but that it has not been easy. The problem? Memory. Vietnam is a wonderful three-dimensional country the rest of the world imagines in two dimensions. Is that fair? Probably not. For the savvy traveller who is more invested in the present than the past, however, Vietnam is an intriguing destination.

We have been to Vietnam many times from the south to the north, from the beaches to the mountains. It is a wonderful country with lush jungles, unspoiled white-sand beaches, colonial cities, a deep spirituality with charming people, and many say the best food in all Asia.

But can you build a new life there rather than just having a glorious holiday? Does it meet our checklist requirements for cost of living, ease of immigration and visas, health care, buying or renting property?

Let's see.

HO CHI MINH CITY (SAIGON)

There are stories around every corner of Ho Chi Minh City—not always happy stories. Lam Son Square is the centre of what was old Saigon. It is dominated by the Opera House, built by the French in the nineteenth century and close to the statue erected on the spot where the Buddhist monk Thich Quang Duc set himself on fire in 1963 to protest the government's persecution of Buddhists. Today, people relax with cocktails on the terrace of the Park Hyatt with no idea of what went on just below them.

That happens a lot in this town, which has more than a few ghosts of the past.

Saigon was a busy Khmer village on the Mekong Delta for centuries, but the Khmer were gradually displaced by the Vietnamese in the 1600s, with Saigon becoming the main port for the south of the country. It was taken over by the French in 1859, and they built an enduring legacy of grand colonial architecture and Parisian Belle Époque style.

After the Japanese occupation ended in 1945, the French boldly came back, but Vietnam rejected another round of colonialism and declared its independence with Ho Chi Minh as its leader. You know the rest of the story: thirty years of war.

Today, as you walk the streets of old Saigon in the morning, the legacy of the French is still evident in the sweet smell of freshly baked croissants and baguettes and how it mixes with the pungent aroma of strong coffee emanating from the stylish cafés. The sidewalks in front of upscale retailers like Gucci and Louis Vuitton are being washed down as piles of plump blue-and-pink hydrangeas by the hundreds are being cut and trimmed for display in the shops. Street vendors are out selling delicate, hand-cut, French-influenced origami cards of Ferris wheels, carousels, and, of course, the Eiffel Tower. The Rex Hotel and its sister, the Caravelle, are still thriving, and it's easy to imagine the French plantation owners of the early 1900s in white linen suits lounging in the sidewalk cafés smoking a fragrant Gauloises and having a small aperitif with their morning coffee.

Rose and Sam

Rose and her partner, Sam, fell in love with Vietnam for just that—"the smell of the place."

Rose explained, "I had been on two holidays in Saigon and I had seen the film *The Quiet American* from the Graham Greene novel. There was something about it I wanted to experience in a deeper way. Living there was the next exciting thing I could do with my life."

Back home, Rose had sold her business and Sam quit his teaching job, and because her kids were grown and independent, there were few ties. At first, she and Sam couldn't get past the usual starting hurdles: Where in Vietnam would they live? Should they buy or rent? What income would they need to live on?

A host of places would have been good for them to settle in, like Hanoi or Hoi An, but Sam was interested in working, and the business climate of Ho Chi Minh City (still Saigon to people our age) suited him best: more action, more opportunities.

The couple prepared themselves well. Before they moved, they studied teaching English as a second language for three months. Their work paid off. Even though they were both over 60, they had little trouble finding teaching jobs in Ho Chi Minh City.

On arrival, they lived in a hotel for a while as they searched for an apartment. "We didn't know where we were going to live, what schools we would target," Rose said. "Our patience paid off as some schools and areas of the city we found were a little too local for us. We decided to live in an upmarket furnished apartment in District 1 versus the established expat area out of town in An Phu."

As she explained, District 1 is downtown, in the heart of the city. It's very gentrified but it is the most expensive real estate in town. All the embassies and consulates are there so you are vying with subsidized government folks for upscale rentals. Their rental cost $5,000 a month, which by local standards was very, very high.

On the other hand, the apartment was palatial: it had three bedrooms, three bathrooms, and an enormous terrace; it was very well appointed throughout and incredibly spacious. They had twenty-four-hour reception, concierge service, a lovely pool, and gardens.

And all they ever needed in the way of shopping and entertainment was literally a few steps away.

Rose admits it was a bit of an embarrassment of riches. But it got even better.

She explained, "We had so much help already, but then one day a charming Vietnamese lady knocked on our door and said, 'I would like to cook and clean for you every day.' I explained that we didn't really need anymore help until she told me it would only cost $150 a month. We agreed and she was just delightful."

Tennis courts were opposite their apartment. Rose and Sam love the game, so they played three mornings a week with their own private tennis coach. A refreshing swim and light breakfast made by their new cook started the day off nicely. They loved wandering through the nearby street markets to buy food and flowers and practise the Vietnamese they were learning. And, apart from their expensive accommodation, everything was cheap.

Sam remembers, "One day I had a giant armful of beautiful orchids, masses of them. I said to Rose, laughing, 'We have to stop spending like this. Look, this just cost us $5!' You just lose track of how relatively inexpensive everything is."

It sounded ideal. For Rose and Sam, it was. The life they enjoyed now was not even thinkable in any city in Canada at any level. Unfortunately, a business commitment brought their experiment in overseas retirement living to a premature end. But their memories endure.

"I could have easily lived in Ho Chi Minh City for the rest of my life," said Rose. Sam agreed.

"You can live well," Sam said. They "bought clothes, food, flowers, ate in the street stalls or the more formal restaurants; they were all so cheap. And the food in Vietnam is just delicious with a touch of French added to the freshest ingredients. We ate out constantly, often at food stalls just sitting at stools.

If it started pouring rain, we would rush to get under a tarpaulin and ended up practising our Vietnamese with everyone else gathered there."

Most importantly, at over 60, they both felt revitalized by the experience. "We used to jump on the back of taxi motorbikes for transport around town," Rose said. "At our apartment, the same man would wait outside for me at 8:30 a.m. and drive me to work. He seemed to know my timetable better than I did. If I was late or early, he would be there waiting."

Rose and Sam went to Vietnam for an adventure; they felt they needed a change to enrich their lives, and enrich it they did.

"I'm a bit of a shy and nervous person," Rose said. "So for me the experience was initially a little bit stressful but ultimately so rewarding."

For Rose and Sam it was a long and welcome break from their routine at home, almost a spiritual awakening.

They left to pursue a business opportunity, arriving back home totally renewed and refreshed. And absolutely ready to do it again.

John and Thanh

Ho Chi Minh City—despite its modern urban appeal—is not your typical idyllic-postcard tropical retreat. It is what it is: a big, busy, noisy, modern city throbbing with activity. That was what attracted John: bored with the life he was living, he craved a more romantic, exciting, and exotic life.

At the age of 62, John, an Australian lawyer, was by most measures a successful man. But he didn't feel that way.

"I'd had an unhappy marriage that ended twenty-five years ago with two adult sons who never really recovered from the family breakup," John said.

"I was bored. I was just representing the same type of criminals all the time: drug traffickers, fraud cases, people trying to take advantage. I was getting to the point where I needed a new challenge in my life." John added, "The life I was leading made me unhealthy. I put on a lot of weight to the point I was concerned about my health."

Then along came a case that changed his life.

It was 2011 and he was representing seven airline attendants who worked for Vietnam Airlines. The Australian Federal Police had arrested them as they were passing through customs to board their flight from Sydney to Ho Chi Minh City. They each had many iPhones and iPads in their flight bags, plus a considerable amount of cash. The police thought the goods and cash were proceeds of a crime.

In the end, there was no crime committed and John won the case, but he never thought for a minute it would change the direction of his life. "The case resulted in me meeting many ordinary Vietnamese people and expats living in Vietnam. The airline people were so grateful that I was invited to visit Ho Chi Minh to stay for an extended holiday."

With the airline case now over, John was drifting back to his old self: stale, unhappy, and unhealthy. He gave the idea of a sabbatical a lot of thought and decided to try it.

"My major concern was that I would become a full-time tourist, which I didn't want. So with the invitation came an opportunity to do some limited legal work, not much but enough to push me to say yes. A working sabbatical sounded perfect."

Even though it wasn't the lower cost of living that inspired John to pack up and take off, it did factor into his decision.

"I decided I would like to run a little legal business on the side in Vietnam, but I never expected I would make close to the same income as I did at home. I didn't need to." John explained that Vietnam is a much different economy than he was used to back home. His expenses here are so low that the savings more than make up for his reduced salary. For example, he said, "in Ho Chi Minh I live in a two-bedroom, fully furnished apartment close to the centre of the city. I pay nine hundred a month in rent. The cost of food here is so low you can eat out every night if you wish. You live very well without having a big income."

John decided to rent out his house back home, and with the rental income and his salary as a lawyer he said he can live very nicely. In fact, John claimed to be in a basic can't-lose situation. Even if "worst comes to worst and I make no money at all here, I'm still ahead."

John's approach to an extended term in Ho Chi Minh City was thoughtfully planned out and smartly executed—a lesson for all of us. Little did he know his new life was about to take another unexpected and life-changing turn.

One day he was having coffee with a business associate and started a conversation with a Vietnamese woman at the next table. Her name was Thanh, and she wanted to practise her English and saw these two foreigners as a good opportunity. At first they didn't think much of each other; he thought she was a chubby-cheeked village girl and she thought John was just "old and fat." But they did meet a few times and eventually, Thanh said, "he stole my heart."

John and Thanh have found real happiness together. And she is not the village hick he labelled her as at their first meeting. She is in her final year of university, the first member of her family to ever get a post-secondary education. Her entire extended family contributed money for her to come to the city and to cover her living expenses while in school. She also assists John with his legal practice and helps him cope with the culture and the formidable Vietnamese bureaucracy.

They are helping each other in other ways too. Thanh is no longer "chubby" and John, says Thanh, is "still old but no longer fat!"

We met John and Thanh on the rooftop terrace of the old Hotel Majestic on the Saigon River. The hotel is like a postcard from the past: a classic white colonial built in 1925 that offered panoramic views over the city and across the river to less developed areas that were alive with Vietcong soldiers in the 1960s. The body-temperature air was moved about by fans while we talked.

John said that, in the end, his decision to move was simply the fact that he could—the timing was right. "I thought, I can do anything I like. I am now at an age where I have done my job as a lawyer. I am reasonably successful. I have no debt. When I came here at sixty-two I really wanted to enjoy the rest of my life, and I was not enjoying it at home."

John found a new and better life in Vietnam. It was more than just a lower cost of living that brought him there; it was the life change that he needed.

HOI AN

It is 520 miles (840 kilometres) north from Ho Chi Minh City to Hoi An on the coast. It might as well be a million. It is that different.

For 1,700 years Hoi An was the centre of the Champa Kingdom and its most powerful port. The town flourished for centuries, attracting traders from far and wide to its booming spice export business. Great trading houses and grand homes were built by the Chinese, the Japanese, the Indians, the Dutch, and finally the French. It was in the mid-nineteenth century, with the French firmly in charge, that Hoi An's long run of prosperity came to an abrupt halt. The town had relied on the Thu Bon River for its shipping needs but it had begun to silt up and, as the ships got bigger, it lost out to the deep-water port of Da Nang, which the French controlled, 18 miles (30 kilometres) up the coast.

Hoi An was largely forgotten and stayed that way for the next 200 years.

During the decades of war with the French and the Americans, the town escaped relatively untouched even while battles raged all around it. Finally, in 1999, it was named a UNESCO World Heritage Site as an example of a preserved fifteenth- to nineteenth-century trading port and for the unique architectural heritage left behind by all the nations that built in their own styles during the town's glory days.

Today you wander the car-free streets of the old town admiring the colourful Chinese lanterns, sampling the wonderful food in the ancient market, and marvelling at the incredible old buildings that now house stylish restaurants and retail shops. Hoi An has its own unique cottage industry as well: custom tailoring. In the old town alone there are 400 tailoring shops big and small. The tailors will create a custom-fit copy of your favourite pair of pants ($30) or construct a new suit from Italian fabric ($200 or less), and do it in a day, or in two days with a proper fitting. The place is a charmer during the day and a kaleidoscope of colour at night.

UNESCO describes Hoi An as
"an example of an exceptionally preserved,
traditional Asian trading port with a history
that dates back to the 2nd century BC."

It is just a mile or so to the powder-sand beaches that run for 18 miles (30 kilometres) north to Da Nang China Beach.

Forty years ago this was the American military landing zone and giant R&R facility. Today those same beaches are dotted with five-star resorts like the Nam Hai, the Hyatt Regency, and, our favourite, the Fusion Maia—a spectacular hotel with a huge spa that offers all the treatments you can fit in for no extra fees beyond your room cost. Sandwiched between the luxurious hotels are condominiums, beachfront villas, and spectacular new golf resorts created by links legends Nick Faldo, Colin Montgomerie, and Greg Norman; spanking new villas line the fairways.

At the Montgomerie Links, Rob, the Irish general manager, took us through villa floor plans and the design of their new beach club. Although it was impressive, we realized this was really a rental property for investors and not a place to live permanently. Yes, it can look and feel like Palm Springs for a fraction of the price and the golf course is stunningly good but with Hoi An 6 miles (10 kilometres) away and Da Nang 12 miles (20 kilometres) in the other direction, you will have to love isolation to consider living here. After a few beers, Rob admitted that he lives in Hoi An for a little over $200 a month, not on the golf property for $300 a day (the price of a mid-size villa rental).

Kevin and Jean

The charms of Hoi An suited Kevin and Jean too. They moved there a year ago after a few years in Vung Tau, a busy expat hangout that is also the port for the offshore oil business 560 miles (900 kilometres) down the coast.

After selling their business at home, they moved to Vietnam for two primary reasons: more adventure and low cost. Jean said without apology, "Our move to Vietnam was pretty selfish really. It was a lifestyle choice."

She explained, "We spend nine months of the year in Hoi An and three months at home to spend Christmas and see family. We would still have to work if we stayed at home. Here we can have a better life and live very comfortably on our investments."

Kevin and Jean left Vung Tau because it felt like they were living in a Western enclave—it is populated by roughneck expats working in the offshore oil business. Now, near Hoi An, they are the only Westerners in a small fishing village and that's the way they like it. "Having said that," added Kevin, "there is plenty of Western contact around as Hoi An and area is a big tourist destination. We also do a bit of work with a friend of ours who heads up an English school that is run out of a hotel here."

Kevin and Jean's living conditions are comfortable if a bit unusual. They rent the bottom floor of a four-storey house—swallows occupy the remainder of the house! The Vietnamese landlord, who lives next door, built the house with the intention of renting out the ground floor and breeding swallows on the top three floors. According to Kevin, the swallows are native to a nearby island but about 200 of the birds were brought here to nest, and every couple of years the owner can harvest the nests—a delicacy in the local cuisine.

"The house is only seven months old," Kevin said. "It has many Western conveniences: two bedrooms, each with an en-suite; a good-sized living area; a terrace; and a nice, new kitchen."

Before you shake your head at the thought of sharing your digs with swallows, these two lovebirds have a three-year lease at $275 a month, and that includes electricity and Wi-Fi.

Plus, the couple said the landlord and his extended family have become good friends.

"He is a great guy," said Kevin warmly. "Last night we were having a cup of tea and the next minute their son, little Bing, comes racing in and says, 'Kevin, Kevin, come, come for food.' They invite us over for a fantastic Vietnamese home-cooked meal several times a week."

Jean agreed. "We also get invited out a lot. The Vietnamese people are very generous and giving, to the point it can get embarrassing. When you go out for dinner, they won't let you pay even though you are in a much better financial position to cover the bill than they are. But no, they just won't let you."

Of course, they admit there are cultural differences that take some getting used to.

Kevin said, "Vietnamese have their own concept of time that isn't ruled by a clock. They are truly lovely people but they work and live at their own pace much of the time. Expats used to keeping to a tight schedule can get pretty exasperated waiting hours, even days for workmen to show up. Even a dinner with local friends arranged for six p.m. might have you cooling your heels until seven thirty, or even later."

Kevin and Jean's two-bedroom apartment costs $275 a month, including electricity and Wi-Fi. The swallows they share the house with are free.

Less stress, less pressure, a much less expensive lifestyle, and more time for relaxing and exploring and just having fun. A few things might take some time getting used to. But for these happy retirees, escaping the rat race and easing into a more congenial lifestyle has been bliss.

As accommodating as it has been, however, Jean and Kevin insist it is the local people and the friendships that they have developed with them that make Hoi An the right choice for them and a much better choice than their former home in Vung Tau. The pace of life is slower and less in your face than in the party town that Vung Tau has become. And their cost of living is still inexpensive.

Kevin marvelled that the nine months a year they live in Hoi An costs them about $32,000 a year *all in* and that includes a holiday trip to a different Southeast Asian country every year.

"This year we went to Laos," said Kevin. "Last year we went to Thailand, and every year we go to Cambodia for a few weeks. And believe me, when we are here, we live extremely well and don't miss out on anything."

So what is a typical day like for them?

"Most mornings we walk to the beach," said Jean, "about two kilometres [1 mile], and I swim about two kilometres and walk back. The beaches are very good here and the water is clean. The sea is usually quite calm except for storms that come up in late October and November. The seafood is always fresh, and dinner for two with a couple of beers is never more than $20 for the two of us."

They golf or play tennis whenever the mood strikes. Or they just wander the countryside, the beach towns, the temples and explore.

"We live such a good life," said Kevin. Jean agreed. In fact, they both feel so refreshed and revived by life in Hoi An that they believe they will live longer—and happier—lives.

OTHER CHOICES: HANOI

Vietnam offers the expatriate a wide variety of places to move to beyond Saigon and Hoi An.

Hanoi, the nation's capital in the north, is a beautiful and refined city sitting on the banks of the Red River. There are four lakes in Hanoi. The largest is Hoan Kiem, and it is the historic and cultural centre of the city. It is surrounded by ancient temples with swan boats (yes, they look like swans) for hire and paths for bicyclists and joggers. The city is abundant with French colonial architecture from its over fifty years as the capital of French Indochina. Tree-lined boulevards, villas and mansions, the Opera House, St. Joseph's Cathedral, and the wonderful Hotel Metropole are images more in keeping with Paris than Asia.

If Ho Chi Minh City is the beating heart, Hanoi is the cool head and the cultural and political epicentre of the country. Until just a few years ago there were no Gucci or Prada stores and the best shopping was in Old Town on one of the original 36 streets, each street dedicated to a particular trade: silk, toys, tin smiths, et cetera. Thankfully, those streets and shops are still there but so are all the flashy world brands and giant shopping malls that are now ubiquitous in every Asian city.

We have been to Hanoi many times in all seasons. Even in the damp and foggy winter period, the city's vivid colours are striking and alive with activity. Year round, the first light of early morning finds hundreds of ping-pong tables and tai chi practitioners crowding the sidewalks and parks around Hoan Kiem Lake in the centre of the city. Hanoi has a rich culinary tradition, having created some of Vietnam's most famous dishes. The most widely known is the wonderful *pho*, the simple rice noodle soup made with rich broth, thinly sliced chicken or beef, bean sprouts, green onion, a sprig of mint, a slice of lime, and a dash of fiery chili paste. It is eaten for breakfast, at street stalls for lunch, and in restaurants for dinner as part of a full meal. *Pho* is to a Vietnamese what a doughnut is to a Canadian.

Modern but simple apartments are available for rent for as little as $500 a month in the central core. Close by is West Lake, where more upscale residences can be rented for $1,500 to $3,000 a month. Just as beautiful as Hoan Kiem, West Lake has a gorgeous new InterContinental hotel and, yes, there are swan boats there too.

Hanoi is only 35 miles (56 kilometres) from the coast, and from there you can take a luxury boat for an overnight cruise to Ha Long Bay, a UNESCO World Heritage Site where massive limestone cones jut out of the waters of the Gulf of Tonkin.

Let us not forget one of the things you are escaping is winter, and Hanoi can be chilly and damp. It is hard to believe on a brisk day in January that it is at exactly the same latitude as Honolulu, Mexico City, and the Sahara Desert.

HUE

In central Vietnam sits the historic city of Hue on the banks of the Perfume River and just a mile or so inland from the South China Sea. Hue rose to prominence as the capital of the Nguyen dynasty that ruled Vietnam from the seventeenth to the nineteenth century. The giant Citadel, occupying an enormous walled compound on the north side of the river, was the seat of power. It was a Forbidden City where only emperors, their concubines, and close associates were allowed access. Today, as yet another UNESCO World Heritage Site, it is open to all and remains a fascinating window to ancient royal life in Vietnam. Although condos are just starting to appear in Hue, it is not yet developed as a retirement destination versus its current tourist orientation.

NHA TRANG

This is *the* beach resort town in South Vietnam, just a fifty-five–minute flight from Ho Chi Minh City and slightly more than that from Hanoi. It is the scuba diving capital of the country and is known for its 3.5-mile-long (6-kilometre) beach that parallels very busy and very touristy Tran Phu Street.

Although development has not been particularly kind to the local beaches, just a short boat ride away to the islands offshore or about a mile north of town you can find pristine white-sand beaches and crystal-clear waters.

Owen and Mai

Owen is a Canadian in his late 50s who made a permanent move to Nha Trang six years ago with his Vietnamese–Canadian wife, Mai. In Canada he had worked for a municipal Ontario government and Mai worked in the provincial health care system.

Owen said, "I had a good job in Canada but as time wore on I felt like a cog in a wheel. I didn't want to just pile on the years after 55 just to maximize the pension and social benefits everybody hangs on for."

A friend of Owen's had a plan to retire early in Vietnam but sadly passed away before he could make the move. Owen decided to implement that same plan for himself and Mai.

Six years later, he and his wife now run a small hotel and, as a Harley-Davidson fanatic, he runs motorcycle tours to the many temples, jungle waterfalls, and gorgeous beaches north of the town. He also publishes a blog that answers questions and provides guidance for people interested in touring or settling in Vietnam.

Retired? Hardly. It sounds like he rarely has a minute to spare, and he loves it.

PROPERTY

Interested in a luxurious apartment facing gorgeous China Beach in Da Nang?

Well, you can buy a one-bedroom terrace suite for $200,000 all the way up to a four-bedroom penthouse for nearly a million dollars. How about an oceanfront villa with massive space, an open plan, and an infinity pool facing the ocean? There are fantastic units being built for $700,000 and up.

No, it's not cheap even if it's five-star. And even if it may sound fairly reasonable by current Toronto or Vancouver standards, beware: there are restrictions regarding foreigners buying property in Vietnam.

For a start, foreigners can purchase apartments only for a maximum lease term of fifty years and they cannot buy land. Plus, the current laws allow for only five specific categories of individuals and organizations to own residences. (See chapter 11.)

These are the categories:

1. People who invest directly in Vietnam or are employed in management positions by domestic or foreign-owned companies in the country.
2. People who receive certificates of merit or medals from the president for their contributions to the country.
3. People who work in socio-economic fields, hold a bachelor's degree or higher, and possess specific specialist skills or knowledge.
4. Foreigners married to Vietnamese nationals.
5. Foreign companies that need to buy homes for their employees posted to Vietnam.

I qualify for none of these, and I suspect hardly any retiree ever will. Vietnamese lawmakers have been debating draft laws that would allow foreigners to buy an apartment and secure leasehold rights for more than fifty years and to buy land as well. None of these things will happen quickly or necessarily deliver everything the drafts contain.

Once again, renting becomes the most viable, the safest, and, we think, the smartest option for living in Vietnam.

That brand-new $200,000 luxury beachfront one-bedroom apartment in Da Nang can be rented for $500 a month or just slightly more for an even higher floor with bigger space.

In the upmarket downtown area of Ho Chi Minh City where Sam and Rose lived, they had a top-floor, super-lux, fully serviced and furnished apartment for a lofty $5,000 a month. A more typical rental of a very nice three-bedroom, furnished place is $1,000 a month. Further away from the cities' influence, rental houses are much less than that, if not always quite as well supported in services for typical Western needs. Typical house rentals in Hoi An or Vung Tau are $500 a month, with electricity and even Wi-Fi included.

COST OF LIVING

As in every Southeast Asian country, you can stay at a gorgeous resort, like the wonderful Nam Hai on China Beach just north of Hoi An, for upwards of $500 a night. But for the permanent or semi-permanent resident, Vietnam can be incredibly inexpensive. Renting a really nice place can be 70 per cent cheaper than Toronto. Restaurant meals can be had for as little as $3 to $5 and a beer is $1.

The trick is to find a place that offers a lifestyle that suits your needs. The two major cities of Ho Chi Minh City and Hanoi have the services expats tend to need, Western-style housing, grocery stores, Wi-Fi, entertainment, and major services.

The countryside is catching up in sophistication but at a much slower rate. It makes up the difference in other ways.

COST OF LIVING

INDICES
Ho Chi Minh City lower than **TORONTO**

CONSUMER PRICES
45%

RENT
68%

RESTAURANT
66%

GROCERIES
52%

Source: numbeo.com

COST OF LIVING

TORONTO vs Ho Chi Minh City

(% lower than Toronto)

Housing

	Toronto	Ho Chi Minh City	% lower
Rent - 3-bedroom apartment city centre	$2,643	$1,037	61%
Rent - 3-bedroom apartment outside city centre	$1,874	$515	73%
Buy - Apartment per 10.75 sq ft (1 sq m) city centre	$6,272	$1,854	70%

Food

Bread	$2.73	$1.16	58%
Eggs	$3.28	$1.42	57%
Chicken breasts	$11.55	$3.57	69%
Tomatoes	$3.21	$0.68	79%

Restaurants

Mid-range meal for two	$60	$18.61	69%
Inexpensive	$12	$2.92	76%

Beer

Domestic	$5.99	$1.06	82%

Taxi

.5 mi (1 km)	$1.78	$0.74	58%
1 hour waiting	$30	$0.96	97%

Utilities

Electricity, heating, water, garbage	$168.13	$78.83	53%

Communications

Internet	$49.73	$16.35	67%
Mobile phone (1 minute prepaid)	$0.25	$0.11	58%

Source: numbeo.com

As Owen said, "There is amazing value for money here in Nha Trang. Bottled water is just fifteen cents, a can of beer is sixty cents, and a big bowl of delicious *pho* filled to the brim is seventy-five cents. My experience is you can live very comfortably here for a thousand a month. For three grand, you can live like a king."

MEDICAL SERVICES

There is no getting around the fact that general medical care to expat standards is not yet as fully developed as in Thailand or Malaysia, particularly outside of the major centres of Ho Chi Minh City and Hanoi.

There are private medical facilities here such as International SOS, which operates three foreign-staffed clinics in Vietnam as well as in over seventy other countries. The costs are much higher than the local care, making medical insurance a must. Local Vietnamese hospitals are inexpensive and competent but the standard of care is basic, the facilities are crowded, and the lack of personnel who speak English can be a problem.

There are 1,000 public hospitals in Vietnam, not nearly enough for a population of over 90 million people. Private hospital groups based in Thailand and Malaysian are expanding their footprint all over Asia and have opened in Ho Chi Minh City and Hanoi. Vinmec, the largest private hospital corporation in Vietnam, is building nine new hospitals to be completed by 2019. Still, 40,000 wealthy Vietnamese went out of country for medical care in 2013. That number is growing as the wealth of the population increases and could soon rival the 70,000 Indonesians who travel annually to just Penang hospitals for medical care. Vietnam will likely be a new medical tourism destination in Asia in just a few years.

Penang, a peaceful and beautiful island off the northwest coast of Malaysia, is a fascinating fusion of East and West.

This new seafront four-bedroom condominium in Tanjung Bungah, a popular expat area north of Georgetown, Malaysia, rents for between $1,500 and $3,000 a month, depending on floor level and view.

JIM HERRLER & ELLEN MA

Canadian authors Jim and Ellen moved from Singapore,
one the world's most expensive cities, to live in charming
and inexpensive Penang, Malaysia.

Jim and Ellen's new luxury condo, with panoramic sea and city
views, 5,800 square feet (540 square metres) of living space, and
shopping and fine dining at their doorstep, rents for $2,500 a month.

Australians Geoffrey and Michael retired to Bali to escape
an underfunded retirement at home.

Geoffrey and Michael's house in Ubud, Bali, is a gorgeous space
built for $65,000, including the land.

This is the backyard of a typical modern Bali villa.

Jimbaran Beach in southern Bali is a popular destination
for feet-in-the-sand seaside dining.

John, an Australian lawyer, retired to Ho Chi Minh City, Vietnam,
and was completely rejuvenated by the place.

© Qui Phung Huynh Vu | Dreamstime.com

Notre-Dame Cathedral in downtown Ho Chi Minh City
(formerly know as Saigon) was built by French colonists
in the late 1800s.

In northern Thailand, Chiang Mai's pace is laid-back, the infrastructure is international, and the landscape is picturesque.

In Thailand, fresh produce is sold daily from these floating markets.

In central Bangkok, Thailand, a fully furnished,
three-bedroom apartment with pool and gym includes…

…a beautiful view over Lumpini Park.

Koh Samui is an idyllic island of natural beauty
and charm in the Gulf of Thailand.

David bought and built his dream house on Koh Samui in 2010 for
$550,000, but luxury condos can be found for much less money.

The government sees the opportunity and already allows and, in fact, encourages foreign-trained doctors to practise in the country.

Our friends Rose and Sam are covered only by travel insurance but found the quality of medical care at doctors' offices and clinics good enough and affordable. The one time they really needed an expat hospital, after Sam had a fall, they went to SOS and had great care by an American doctor.

Owen and Mai have had good care as well. "In Canada," he said, "getting an MRI took four months. At a Thai-run private hospital in Ho Chi Minh City I got one same day. I had the scan ten minutes after arriving, on a brand-new machine, and my results were read by a foreign-trained, English-speaking doctor immediately. I was out the door in less than an hour with a bill for $25 for the scan and $5 for the doctors' consult. Try doing that in Canada."

We won't. On the other hand, do keep in mind that the Ho Chi Minh City clinic is a *five-hour plus* drive from Sam's home in Nha Trang.

> *"I had an MRI at a Thai-run hospital in*
> *Ho Chi Minh City on the day I arrived.*
> *The results were read by a foreign-trained,*
> *English-speaking doctor and the bill was $30."*

To live in a developing country like Vietnam and have no medical or evacuation insurance at all is a risk. If the local medical services can't manage your serious illness or catastrophic injury, you will need evacuation to Singapore, Bangkok, or Malaysia and that costs tens of thousands of dollars, plus the cost of treatment in any of those cities.

There is no doubt at all that across the board Southeast Asia has many of the best and least expensive opportunities in the world; health, however, is one area of your life that you cannot afford to risk. What we recommend is that whatever type of residency you choose—permanent or semi-permanent—you invest in the best international, private health insurance you can afford. Remember, even if you are a part-time resident and maintain your Canadian coverage, it is still necessary to carry a travel policy that allows for medical evacuation. (See chapter 9.)

VISAS AND IMMIGRATION

Visas in Vietnam are, on the one hand, simple to obtain and, on the other, a bit of a concern to some expats as the immigration services in general have not caught up with the more sophisticated expansionary aspects of the country. There is no twelve-month multiple-entry visa available and no retirement visa has yet been introduced. Therefore, expats are all on three- to six-month tourist visas. These are easily renewed in-country up to four times before an exit stamp is required. You simply exit a border and return to a new, renewable tourist visa. Every expat is required to register with the police but that is common in many Asian countries. Everyone in Vietnam, whether expat or local, is registered. People we interviewed say there are no issues with either getting the visas or renewing them. Some use an agent, some don't; it is certainly not a requirement, just a convenience. All easy enough, but there is a degree of uncertainty that comes with a dated process that should and likely will be replaced down the road. (See chapter 10 for details.)

Tips and Traps: Vietnam

1. Vietnam offers an array of lifestyles from city life in Hanoi or Ho Chi Minh City to the more laid-back Hoi An or the beach life of Da Nang. You will not be alone. Many foreigners have discovered Vietnam's charms.

2. The food is sensational and incredibly cheap. Never fear eating at street stalls. Food and food preparation is fresh and clean everywhere. This isn't China.

3. Roll with it. The Vietnamese concept of time is different than ours. They are an overly generous and warm people. Accept their generosity and reciprocate when you can.

4. Vietnamese *love* foreigners. There is absolutely no animosity toward Westerners for the French and American wars that ravaged the country.

5. Ho Chi Minh City's downtown core is a mecca for pickpockets and purse-snatchers. Only carry what you need. Other than that one location, crime is very rare and violent crime almost non-existent in the entire country.

6. Visas are not available for long-term stays and must be renewed every three months in most cases. Bit of a hassle but generally problem-free.

7. Medical care is good enough for most situations and better in larger cities and at the international clinics. Expats should have private health coverage that allows for medical evacuation. When all is said and done, basic needs can be well met and very cheaply too.

FINAL THOUGHT

We love Vietnam. However, as a sophisticated expat retirement destination for Canadians, it is not yet in the same league as other Southeast Asian options such as Malaysia or Thailand. We considered it for ourselves but felt it wasn't quite as developed as we wanted. As I am in my mid-60s I want top-quality health care now, not down the road. I want a large community of expats and I want Western-style services to be there when I want them. A box of Raisin Bran, in my view, should not be seen as a luxury item. As we have said before in the book, some destinations are ready for expat retirees, of any age, right now. Vietnam will be a country to watch in the next few years. It has the potential to be the next great retirement destination in Southeast Asia. For the moment, we think it is best suited to a younger, more entrepreneurial, more adventurous crowd.

THE CHECKLIST

1. Cost of living: Generally very inexpensive but can go as high as you want to rent property in cities. Food cheap, restaurants cheap, all services very cheap. Thumbs up.
2. Buying or renting: Very hard to buy unless you meet strict criteria. Easy to rent and very good value. Thumbs up.
3. Health care: Local care adequate for expats. Private insurance and medical evac required. Thumbs partly up.
4. Visas and immigration: Still third world but not difficult. Thumbs partly up.

chapter 7

Cambodia:
The Ruby in the Rough?

ambodia has an untamed quality that has drawn adventurers for centuries. For those susceptible to its magic, it transfixes you and digs deep into your soul.

You might get hooked. Some retirees already have!

Perhaps the appeal is due to the intoxicating heat, where a house plant grows to the size of a tree, or to the Mekong River—the country's heartbeat. One of the truly great river systems in the world, the Mekong gets its start high in the Himalayas and flows through China, Myanmar, Laos, Thailand, Cambodia, and Vietnam. Through time, this wide, muddy river has seen so much joy, pleasure, pain, and cruelty.

Cambodia occupies the centre of Indo-Chine, a term that refers to French Indo-China, which, from the late 1800s until the mid-1950s, included Vietnam, Cambodia, and Laos.

Cambodia

The Vietnamese and the Laotians both suffered terribly under the French and then again with the subsequent arrival of the Americans. But the Cambodians were treated the most harshly of all. They were mere pawns in a power game, and it was a game played with B-52 bombers at 30,000 feet that they had no say in. Back in the early 1970s, theirs was no fight for sovereignty and independence like the Vietnamese. As one of the poorest countries in the world, Cambodia was just trying to get by every day.

Twice as many bombs were dropped on Cambodia during the Vietnam War through 1975 as were dropped on Japan during all of the Second World War. Tens of thousands of innocents were killed, villages decimated, and a rural economy reduced to ruins. All of this was the illegal secret war promoted by Washington to destroy any potential safe haven for Communists, even if none of any consequence were ever found there.

And it got worse because then came the Khmer Rouge. This was the name—French for the Red Khmers—given to the followers of the Communist Party of Kampuchea in Cambodia. Formed in 1968 as an offshoot of the North Vietnamese Army, it ruled Cambodia from 1975 to 1979. After years of battling the government forces, they stormed into the capital Phnom Penh in 1975 and set about liquidating—through mass murder, torture, starvation, and untreated disease—about 2 million of their own countrymen. No one knows the exact number.

The hallmarks were the Killing Fields and the torture and extermination centres—more than one hundred in all—set up all over the country. People were force-marched out of the cities to work as slave labour in the fields with no medical care, no food, no housing.

It was an unbelievable, ideologically driven form of madness with no point or purpose.

The Khmer Rouge was defeated, largely due to the intervention of the Vietnamese, in 1979. Instability remained all the way through to 1997, when former Khmer Rouge commander Hun Sen wrested control from his former co-premier Prince Norodom Ranariddh to become sole prime minister; he holds that position to this day. The killing had ended and some form of normalcy has returned to the country.

Cambodia is still known for rampant corruption, human trafficking, and poverty levels second only to North Korea in Asia. Income levels are 50 per cent of Vietnam and only 20 per cent of that of Thailand; this, despite an economy that has grown an average of 6 per cent annually for ten years. Even with the Khmer Rouge long gone, life is hard in Cambodia.

Today, when you are in the country it is impossible to understand how such a gentle and peaceful people could have perpetrated these horrors. It feels like the whole episode was a dream, and it is difficult to reconcile how such insanity and cruelty could take over a country and its entire population for two decades.

Most importantly to all of us, that terrible cruelty is history now. Still, there is no doubt that today's Cambodia has a raw, edgy 1960s–era Indo-Chine authenticity about it. And that is its appeal.

Today, the Cambodian people are desperate to move on from those terrible times, and your warm welcome from them will be at least the equal of any Southeast Asian country.

Cambodia resonates with its French colonial past as much as it does with its legacy of inhumanity and war. It is the closest you can get to how Southeast Asia would have felt in the 60s. Pedal-powered cyclos still fill the streets but are being replaced by motorized tuk-tuks. The smells of strong coffee and warm baguettes fill the morning air. You can buy marijuana-laced

"Happy" pizzas all along the banks of the Mekong in Phnom Penh or be up at the crack of dawn to watch the sunrise at Angkor Wat with about 5,000 other tourists with the same idea.

All these retro moments strung together can trigger a love affair with the country. It is different from the attractions of any other place in Asia and, perhaps, inexplicable to those who haven't sampled its vibrant new life.

Janet and Rick

It was this confusing but deep attraction that attracted Janet and Rick. They first visited Phnom Penh a decade ago and it has kept a hold on them ever since.

Janet said, "We didn't choose to live in Cambodia; it chose us. I found it simply intoxicating every time we returned here."

"I don't recall the moment we made the decision to move to Cambodia," added Rick. "It just happened. We built the house as Janet was coming here for a month or two every year for work."

Janet said that she likes the unpredictability of life in Cambodia. "At home you know you will be getting on a bus every Monday morning, in the rain or snow or whatever. You pretty much know what's going to happen day in, day out." She paused and smiled reflectively. "Here, you wake up in the morning and you have no idea what is in store. You want to leave the house but you can't because there is a one-ton water buffalo in the way." She laughed. "There is electricity or there isn't—which I find very frustrating but sometimes exhilarating as well."

They are both enchanted by the rich Khmer Cambodian culture.

Janet said one only has to visit Angkor Wat to understand that. Janet admits up front that Cambodia—like Vietnam—has had a difficult time getting past its past. I suggested that most

Canadians probably have a negative image of Cambodia. They both nodded.

But in many ways, they could not disagree more. Cambodia is no cultural wasteland.

"There are films, concerts, and plays," said Janet. "There are art openings and live performances. There are two local websites—one on music, what is on this week, and one on the art scene. And it is just incredible! You actually cannot keep up with it all. There are book clubs, choirs, a lot of live music, and the restaurants, my God, the restaurants are wonderful."

Angkor Wat is one of seventy-two principal temples in the area outside the town of Siem Reap. In 2013 over 2 million visitors visited the 900-year-old site.

Janet and Rick live in a traditional Khmer-style house set on poles on land adjacent to the Mekong River. Their house is less than thirty minutes' drive from the centre of the city. Wide verandas watch over the expanse of the muddy Mekong. There are ducks in the garden, even a local goat. In the wet season, the Mekong laps at their front lawn and occasionally comes up right under their house—but that's why it is on poles, and the deluge rarely lasts long.

When we visited it was the end of the wet season. The Mekong is swollen by both tropical rains and by the snowmelt high up in the Himalayas in China, the source of the river. Add to that, water pouring in from Burma, Laos, Thailand, and the rest of Cambodia and it becomes the world's twelfth-longest river system.

It is here, in this house they had built by the river, that Janet and Rick spend leisurely days and warm dreamy nights. The ceiling fans slowly turn, the staff brings tea and coffee.

They also have a driver, gardeners, and house cleaners. It is as close as you get to the old days when the French colonized Indo-Chine. Not that Janet and Rick are at all exploitive. In fact, they continue to employ a large number of staff more out of concerns for their well-being than their own need for household help. Relative to the poverty around them, they are undoubtedly privileged. They know this only too well.

Janet and Rick not only have a great lifestyle, but also a meaningful life. Both are semi-retired: Janet is a part-time university lecturer and Rick is in IT. They are both deeply involved with the Cambodian people and helping to move them from their unhappy past to a more positive future.

When they built their house in 1999, Janet was still travelling regularly to Cambodia for work. Janet said, "We had become deeply interested, enmeshed in the Cambodian people, relationships, and culture. We were pretty engaged in our village.

"At first we didn't say we were coming to Cambodia to stay. We built the house with friends because we were coming frequently. Our friends were already here, and it sounded like a good thing to do. It was fun to build, and we thought we couldn't lose on it. Then my mother came here in 2000 and stayed for a month or two. She was quite elderly at the time, eighty-three, and said to me one day, 'Now I understand why you will never come back.'"

Janet said she was taken aback. It was about that time that they began talking about a more permanent arrangement.

"Several friends of our age have brought their elderly parents—in three cases we know—to Phnom Penh, and they have had a really wonderful end to their days living here. Living with their children in a different situation with lots of support and all the care they would ever need—it is a million times better than what they could ever get at home."

And not too much longer after that, the final domino fell. They made the move. It has been a great life for them. Ironically, having found themselves relocated to Cambodia, they both feel excited about the future—wherever they end up.

"Will we stay forever?" asked Janet rhetorically. "Yes and no. Nothing lasts forever." They both smile confidently. For now, Cambodia is home and they couldn't be happier.

It is here, in their house on the Mekong, that Janet and Rick spend leisurely days and warm, dreamy nights. The fans slowly turn, the staff who run the house bring cold drinks, the gardens are immaculately tended, and their full-time driver takes them wherever they need to go.

Cambodia is not a common destination for expats. There are reasons. Cambodia is a more difficult environment to adjust to than Thailand or Malaysia, which is commonly referred to as Asia Lite. People are not as knowledgeable about Cambodia, unlike its more familiar and developed neighbours, and then there are likely reservations because of the terrible war and cruelty endured by the country through the 70s and 80s. The name given to the area just outside Phnom Penh where hundreds of thousands were executed—the Killing Fields—still resonates.

This still annoys Janet.

"It is taking so long for the country to shed this image. The people don't want it. They want to go beyond that. They don't want Cambodia to just be the Killing Fields anymore. Apart from the genocide itself, which was appalling, every foreign press article about Cambodia has the obligatory paragraph: Hun Sen, former Khmer Rouge strongman, authoritarian, da, da, da.

That is the boilerplate that just gets dumped in. You just can't get an unbiased view of what is going on here without that prism to look through. To describe Hun Sen as former Khmer Rouge is unfair—he risked his life to get rid of them and without him they would not be gone today. It is just the wrong cast. Some elements [are correct], yes, but it is just so judgmental."

Rick added, "So much of this country was born after all that time anyway. Yes, these old men who did these terrible things should be punished under the law but not their children."

War has deeply marked Cambodia. This is too hard to scrub from history, and the Killing Fields are always there to remind those who are tempted to forget.

Jon Swain, a journalist who lived in Cambodia in the early 1970s and was lucky to be trucked out by the Khmer Rouge in 1975 rather than be executed, can't seem to let go of Cambodia. In his book, *River of Time,* he talks of how the Mekong itself holds so much of this meaning. "There is something about the Mekong itself, which, even years later, makes me want to sit down beside it and watch my whole life go by."

Even though the river brings so much life and feeds all the lands of Indo-China, Swain says, "For myself there are certain things I shall never forget: the bodies I saw being tossed about in its violent eddies in the early morning mist when the Mekong is at its most majestic and mysterious. Or the day when a Khmer Rouge general marched his soldiers behind a screen of Vietnamese civilians into the waiting guns of the Viet Cong in a border skirmish. 'It's a new form of psychological warfare,' the general said as the bodies dropped in front of him." But, Swain still loves Cambodia. "What carries me back to the place of my dreams are those first days [when I arrived]." He came from a bleak, grey, cold Paris winter and burst into the tropical heat of Phnom Penh. "I felt as if I had entered a beautiful garden. As I stepped off the Air France 707 onto the sticky hot tarmac of Pochentong airport, I was beginning a new life. I forgot about Paris and began an adventure and love affair with Indo-China to which I have been faithful ever since."

The times got bleaker in the 1970s as the terror of the Khmer Rouge came closer to the city. A popular hotel for expatriates and journalists back then, as now, was Le Royal, now called Raffles Hotel Le Royal. As tensions built, the behaviour of the expat journalists became more and more risqué. War does that to people. Swain tells of "eerie occasions of forced humor and horseplay in the pool." Even the pool's broken water filtration system causing the water to badly need a change did not stop one female photographer making love to two men on the same night, one in the deep end and one in the shallow end, to general applause.

Phnom Penh has changed a lot. Le Royal has regained its grandeur and the pool is sparkling.

PHNOM PENH

The capital of Cambodia, Phnom Penh, is located on the banks of the Mekong, Tonle Sap, and Bassac rivers. It still echoes with the feel of Old Asia, but it also has a new and exciting aspect to it. Phnom Penh is changing rapidly, and for the Westerner, the comforts of modern life are fast appearing.

Ted and Helen

Ted and Helen, who are in their late 50s, came to Cambodia thirteen years ago and run a restaurant and bar in the upmarket downtown area of Boeung Keng Kang 1 (commonly referred to as BKK1). Helen said, "We were lucky in terms of the period we were here—2000 to now. It is a long time and we have seen a lot of changes, particularly in the last five years. Big corporations coming in bringing more wealth. Between 2000 and 2004, it didn't change much at all."

But Helen added that, sadly, a lot of the "soul of the city" and the old edginess is gone.

Safety was an issue back then, although Helen is pretty nonchalant about it. "It was still safe then because you didn't go where the problems were—you would get a text message that there had been a hand grenade thrown here or a shooting there and you just didn't go into those areas. But all of that is gone now except for the occasional instance of army commanders shooting up karaoke bars."

What has changed, Helen said, is that it is more modern, cleaner, more accessible, and much safer. "There is a lot of investment in the city, and the landscape has changed dramatically. The division of rich and poor is getting bigger but the middle class is growing too."

There is a dark side to development, she added.

"When we first came here, the city was rich with old French architecture, extraordinary but rundown. Now, a lot of that has been destroyed for new development. You get really angry about it, plus the sex trafficking, the high incidence of unpunished rape, the terrible environmental degradation of unrestricted logging."

The contrasts between good and evil are still very apparent here. Now it's economic, though, and not military.

Ted and Helen have seen a recent influx of couples appearing recently rather than the usual singles crowd. "We have met a lot more couples in the last few years, mostly Americans who often work from home, travelling through Southeast Asia to find a place to live. They want a new life and lifestyle." Ted added that a lot of them end up choosing Thailand or Malaysia over Cambodia in the end. "You have to be a certain character to get on in Cambodia. It is an edgy experience for a first-timer in Asia."

Still, it is increasingly on the radar for expats.

"Almost everybody who comes here wants to stay and they almost always come back," said Helen. "We meet people who say, 'I was here five years ago, I always wanted to return,' or people here for the first time saying, 'Oh, I had no idea it would be this nice.'"

As visitors to a country, we all have to be careful not to moralize or judge the culture, and that includes less savoury aspects of a culture. In Cambodia, as in many parts of Southeast Asia, that includes the sex tourism industry, which is just part of the landscape here. But when you've lived in a country like Cambodia as long as Helen and Ted, you develop strong opinions.

Helen doesn't think the country is suitable for couples and certainly not retirees. In her frank manner she explained, "Ninety per cent of the time the males will get 'rice fever.' Guaranteed. Six of my girlfriends have left this year—all turned 40—all single. They left for two reasons—their careers and no men. It really is a desert for foreign women. And Cambodia can be really tough to adjust to. It's not like moving to Chiang Mai or Bangkok."

Cambodia is still "old" Asia. Although it does have some new and modern elements, it remains one of the few places you can experience what colonial life was like under the French over seventy years ago.

Garry and Rita

Despite Helen's rather negative point of view, we found another couple living very happily in Cambodia: Garry and Rita.

Their shift to Cambodia was driven by factors other than retirement or the need for a change. It was a move of necessity based on the need to work. It is a story that fits with many people working in the West who are over 50 years of age.

As Rita explained, "Garry is in marketing, and when he got to age fifty the company bosses told him they really didn't have anything for him in the future. But if he would move to Southeast Asia, they would give him a twelve-month contract to expand the business. That was five years ago, and the business is still expanding."

Garry was told he could locate the company's office anywhere in Southeast Asia. He and Rita chose Phnom Penh and are now sure they made the right decision. Garry believes that other cities like Hanoi, Ho Chi Minh City, Kuala Lumpur, Singapore, Bangkok, and Jakarta are just big and relatively much more expensive.

He said, "When you boil it all down, it gets to just a few really inexpensive places. Cambodia is one, Vientiane [in Laos] is another—but there are issues with Vientiane and with Laos. Thailand is fine—if you get out of Bangkok. A lot of our friends have retired to Krabi in Thailand. Penang is another good place.

"But Cambodia is old Asia—still intact, the way it used to be. It is exotic. It has the French colonial feel and architecture. It is, to me, the way Hanoi used to be twenty-five years ago. Cambodia is not suddenly going to get ambitious, because the Cambodian people are not ambitious like the Vietnamese or Thais. Not lazy, just laid-back in their style. They are more like Laotians."

The Laotians, according to Garry, were recently voted the happiest people in the world. He cited the example of a cab driver who might take three fares in one day and decide that is enough—he is happy with what he earned and will take the afternoon off to drink with his mates.

Well, Garry may think that is just laid-back but lazy does come to mind.

Rita is aware that corruption and human rights violations in Cambodia remain real problems. This concerns her but she said, "Let's say you are totally self-serving and the things you love to do are to eat great food, drink good wines, have a beautiful place to live—all for very little money. Then you have lots of cheap domestic help and never have to wash a dish or clean a toilet. If that appeals, Phnom Penh offers all of this and more."

That's not exactly the humanitarian point of view endorsed by the likes of Angelina Jolie. Rita knows that. Cambodia, however, is not the country for everyone and absolutely not the right fit for anyone who doesn't have a thick skin.

People like Garry and Rita admit that one of the issues retirees need to come to terms with is the idea that living in the West creates certain expectations about the way people should live. Basic services in Cambodia are cheap compared to cities like Toronto and Vancouver or Calgary or Montreal—absurdly so in some categories—and the concern might be that the people are being exploited. Expats we talked with admit that is what it could look like … from where outsiders sit. But once you live inside a country, you begin to understand that life is lived differently. In fact, we might go so far as to suggest that the average Canadian retiree is less respected and more exploited than the average Cambodian of the same age.

Garry and Rita live in the Western-dominated part of Phnom Penh, BKK1. It is full of great restaurants that are very comfortable and affordable. They rent a large two-storey house that is spacious and luxurious. Rita is shocked by the pace of change in the city: "Relative to when we came here four and a half years ago, I cannot tell you the number of world-class restaurants and gorgeous little back-street bars that have opened. I can take you to twenty new places where you could walk in and feel like you were in Toronto or Melbourne or even New York or Paris."

PROPERTY

Despite the recent influx of foreigners and offshore property investment dollars, renting in Cambodia is still very inexpensive by any Western standard.

The area in Phnom Penh where Garry and Rita live is upmarket; the neighbourhood has tree-lined streets, larger homes, serviced apartments, and myriad restaurants to choose from. Rent ranges from $2,000 to $3,000 a month for a large, pleasant, fully furnished house with a garden.

Alan pays $600 a month in rent for his apartment. At his previous place, the top half of an old house in the centre of town he describes as beautiful, he paid $450 a month. But, he pointed out, even that was expensive. "A lot of the staff at *The Post* would be paying $200 to $250 a month for a furnished and air-conditioned apartment," said Alan.

He would buy a property now if he had the money. "Owning property here would be a long-term investment, not a quick flip. Tourism is going to explode, and the politics is steadily settling down to a more business-oriented dynamic."

Alan added, "What you see in Cambodia now is what I saw in Thailand thirty-five years ago. This place is just starting to open up and take off. If people want to visit or stay in the real Southeast Asia, it is here in the countryside of Cambodia. People are living just like they did two thousand years ago. Not much has changed: they still use buffalos to plough their fields and you don't see that in Thailand anymore. You see it here."

The option of buying property is very affordable for foreigners. A pleasant two-bedroom apartment in central Phnom Penh costs between $50,000 and $300,000 for very high end. Outside the city proper, it is significantly cheaper.

Alan told us, "I have an American friend—a professional tennis coach—who bought a block of land and built a house on a hillside in Kep with ocean views." He said the land, the house, everything, cost the friend $25,000. It isn't a palace, he admits, but basic Khmer style with two bedrooms on stilts. It has power and water tanks and is ten minutes from the beach. He said that quite a few foreigners have moved into that area.

Kep is a charming beach village five hours' drive from Phnom Penh. It was Cambodia's top seaside destination until Sihanoukville on the south coast eclipsed it in the 1960s. But today it is enjoying a renaissance, especially among wealthy Cambodians, partly because Sihanoukville has fallen into disrepute as a sex-pat destination. Kep has over one hundred old and abandoned French villas that are architecturally stunning and holding up well despite their age, over fifty years for most of them. They are reputed to be mostly owned and loosely kept up by Cambodian military officials who are waiting for prices to rise to sell them off to foreigners. Some rules will need to be broken to do that.

Expats can own freehold property in Cambodian buildings only above the ground floor. This works well for apartments or even older buildings with several levels such as the upper floors of a shop house. The intention of the law is that foreigners cannot own land or houses, only apartments. But we are in Asia, and the intention of the law is often circumvented.

Kep has over one hundred gorgeous old French villas in the hills over the beach, some from the 1930s. All seem to be abandoned but, in truth, they are quietly maintained, waiting for the day when property laws loosen and they can be sold.

We would never suggest skirting the rules, in any Southeast Asian country. It can cause a lot of problems over time. We are of the view that you keep it simple. If you do want to buy, protect your investment by following the law, buying above ground floor, and always making sure you get the best possible legal advice about the purchase.

COST OF LIVING

The magic of Cambodia struck Joanna as soon as she visited Phnom Penh over twenty years ago. "I fell in love with the place right away," she said, "and I'm still trying to work out why. I would go to a village and see that there was a cycle to growing rice and it meant something to me. Maybe it is the connection with the cycle of life and nature, maybe it's the delightful people; I still don't know."

Joanna rents a two-bedroom apartment above a café. It is in the centre of town, right opposite the old palace wall and on a tree-lined street. She leases it from the British owner of the café below for just over $1,000 a month. It's about average for the area. "Prices vary but in the centre, where I am and which is very popular, it is a bit more expensive. I like this

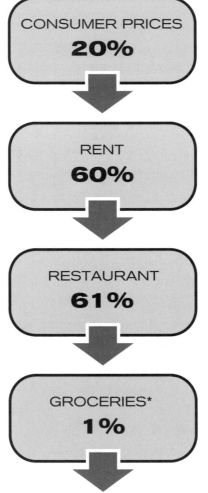

COST OF LIVING

INDICES

Phnom Penh lower than **TORONTO**

CONSUMER PRICES
20%

RENT
60%

RESTAURANT
61%

GROCERIES*
1%

* Grocery index skewed due to very high cost of imported items that appear on the Numbeo grocery list. Locally sourced grocery items are 50 to 75% cheaper than in Toronto.

Source: numbeo.com

lovely street so much, right next to the old palace wall, and it is a delightful mix of Cambodians and foreigners."

Joanne believes her rent is "up there."

"Some things cost more. Gasoline is expensive, but I bought my car for $5,000 ten years ago and it is still worth three or four. Things keep their value here."

However, she quickly added that other costs of living are super low. "Vegetables are incredibly cheap. I go into a little shop and buy three days' worth for three dollars. Fruit is a bit more but only five dollars for three days' worth." Electricity costs are low given she runs air conditioning all the time in the hot months and she has a full suite of appliances. Her electric bill is between $45 and $95 a month. "Mobile phones are very cheap, as are landlines," Joanna said. "On my landline it is just a couple of dollars for a half-hour long distance call and internet is just ten dollars a month."

Joanna estimates that, for her, the cost of living in Cambodia is about a quarter of what it would cost in Canada. She also has a part-time helper, cleaning and cooking, for less than $100 a month.

The cost of living well in Phnom Penh is, in fact, about 60 per cent or less of what it would cost to live in Toronto. Grocery prices are about 40 per cent lower, restaurant prices are more than 70 per cent cheaper, and rent is almost 75 per cent cheaper.

Alan Parkhurst, a long-time resident of the city and editor of the *Phnom Penh Post*, told us: "A beer is never more than a dollar a bottle. Spirits and beer are cheaper here than I can buy duty free anywhere in the world. There is no tax on alcohol."

Alan believes that a single person can easily live on $1,000 a month. For Joanna it is about $2,000 a month, while Ted says a couple could live very comfortably, all in, for $3,000 a

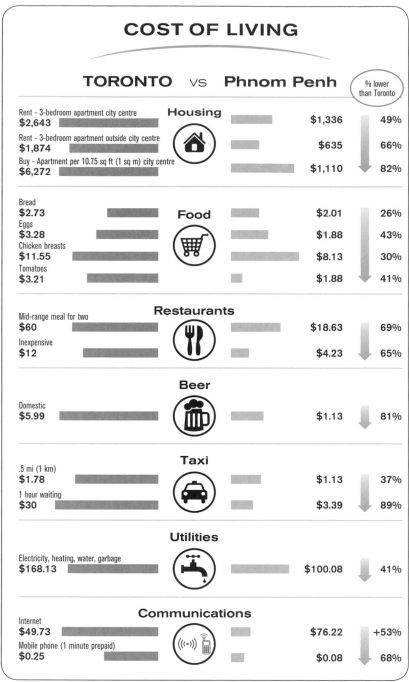

COST OF LIVING

TORONTO vs Phnom Penh

% lower than Toronto

Housing

Rent - 3-bedroom apartment city centre
$2,643 — **$1,336** — 49%

Rent - 3-bedroom apartment outside city centre
$1,874 — **$635** — 66%

Buy - Apartment per 10.75 sq ft (1 sq m) city centre
$6,272 — **$1,110** — 82%

Food

Bread
$2.73 — **$2.01** — 26%

Eggs
$3.28 — **$1.88** — 43%

Chicken breasts
$11.55 — **$8.13** — 30%

Tomatoes
$3.21 — **$1.88** — 41%

Restaurants

Mid-range meal for two
$60 — **$18.63** — 69%

Inexpensive
$12 — **$4.23** — 65%

Beer

Domestic
$5.99 — **$1.13** — 81%

Taxi

.5 mi (1 km)
$1.78 — **$1.13** — 37%

1 hour waiting
$30 — **$3.39** — 89%

Utilities

Electricity, heating, water, garbage
$168.13 — **$100.08** — 41%

Communications

Internet
$49.73 — **$76.22** — +53%

Mobile phone (1 minute prepaid)
$0.25 — **$0.08** — 68%

Source: numbeo.com

month. Despite personal variations, it is clear that living in Cambodia is well within reach of Canadians, especially retirees who are watching their budget.

> *"What I see in Cambodia now is what I saw in Thailand thirty-five years ago. The place is just starting to open up, but if people want to live in the real Southeast Asia, it is here in the countryside of Cambodia. People still live as they did 2,000 years ago."*

MEDICAL SERVICES

There is no question that general medical services of a Western standard are largely absent in Cambodia. The health system has all the inconsistencies you would expect of third world locales, and just like in Vietnam and Bali, a serious illness often means that you have to travel to Singapore, Malaysia, or Thailand. And, of course, if you are too ill or injured to travel and you do not have medical evacuation coverage, you could be in deep financial trouble—something an older retiree or anyone on a budget will not want to face.

Again, as we have said about other countries, the sensible path is that you carry health insurance and medical evacuation insurance if at all possible. However, we were surprised at some of the positive experiences people had with health care and it will get better as infrastructure and property investments ramp up.

Joanna has no health insurance. At over 70 years of age, she would find it hard to get anyway. Recently she became very ill and had to be treated locally. She told us, "I had a bacterial

infection in my leg. It was cellulitis. That can be quite dangerous. I had a high fever and chills. I got an appointment with
an Australian doctor and he diagnosed it right away. He drew
a circle on my leg around the infection and while we discussed
which hospital to go to, it had spread outside the circle!" She
was admitted to a French Cambodian clinic and treated by
three doctors—two French and one French Cambodian. She
was there ten days on an antibiotic drip and it cost her very
little. A stay at an International SOS facility might have been
better, she admitted, but it would have cost much more.

Janet and Rick recognize that the medical situation is a
real issue but they too have no private health care coverage.
Again, we found this a very risky decision and said so.

Janet understood but explained.

"We both came here with health insurance from a Hong
Kong insurance group, but we decided it wasn't worth it."
Janet recently had heart surgery in Sydney but it was a planned
procedure and not an emergency. "We paid for it up front as
an overseas patient and it cost $45,000. The way we looked at
it, it is ten years of health insurance."

Garry and Rita have medical evacuation insurance and a
million-dollar U.S. medical policy. This costs them only $1,400
a year at the moment but Garry warns it will skyrocket when
he hits 60 next year.

Alan said most people go to Bangkok or Vietnam for private hospital medical care. But he added, "It is getting a lot
better here. A couple of big Thai hospitals have been built and
they are quite good. And SOS is here if you need it."

Cambodia's flagship international hospital is Calmette, a
government-run medical centre on Monivong Boulevard in
Phnom Penh. Funded by the Cambodian and French governments, it is a fee-for-service facility targeted at both locals and

expats that offers good-quality, affordable medical care. The 250-bed hospital provides a full range of medical services such as surgical, obstetrics, radiology, and microbiology.

In Siem Reap, near the famous ruins of Angkor Wat, the Royal Angkor International Hospital provides a high standard of medical care. It is owned and operated by Thailand's Bangkok Hospital Group. Patients, however, are required to pay in cash or with private medical insurance.

Our conclusion: we were surprised at some of the positive medical experiences of the people we interviewed. Quality care is still location specific (Phnom Penh and Siem Reap), and it is expensive, often requiring cash to cover the bill.

VISAS AND IMMIGRATION

Visas are currently no barrier to retiring and living in Cambodia. The situation could change, however, if only because of the rapid political and economic developments underway in the country.

Most visitors to Cambodia obtain a thirty-day tourist visa for $22. These can be obtained on arrival at Phnom Penh and Siem Reap airports and at land borders. One passport-sized photo is all that is required along with foreign currency, preferably U.S. dollars.

With the tourist visa you are allowed to extend your stay, just once, for an extra thirty days at a cost of about $50. If you intend to stay longer, it is best to apply for an ordinary visa, often referred to as a business visa. Like a tourist visa, this is valid for thirty days but can be extended indefinitely.

You can extend your stay from within the country, so there is no need to leave. You have the option to extend for one, three, six, or twelve months. The one- and three-month visas will allow you only a single entry, which means every time you leave the country, you need a new visa.

Alan said, "I just pay an agent the three hundred a year and get a new visa. You can do it through any travel agent here. I know people who have lived here for years and have never left the country. Cambodia is the easiest place in Southeast Asia to stay long term."

Tips and Traps: Cambodia

1. Cambodia provides an adventure, not just a retirement. Be aware, it is fascinating but edgy. There are other destinations with many more comforts.
2. Although it is infamous for the Khmer Rouge and the horrors they inflicted on the populace, these events are history now. It shouldn't scare you away.
3. Cambodia is the last vestige of the Southeast Asia of the 1970s. Charming it can be but it still has a dark side of corruption, prostitution, human trafficking, and drug running. Carry or keep in your vehicle just the cash or single credit card you need.
4. English is surprisingly widely spoken in Cambodia. Learning the basics of the Khmer language will be appreciated.
5. Cambodia is fabulously inexpensive.
6. General medical facilities are of a lesser standard compared to Malaysia or Thailand and are very location specific. Basic needs are met, and there are some good facilities recently built in the major centres.

7. By law foreigners can buy only apartments above the ground floor. Renting, however, is extremely inexpensive, and there is a wide range of comfortable options available, from traditional Khmer housing to French colonial townhouses to modern serviced apartments.

FINAL THOUGHT

Cambodia is a fantastic country despite it tragic history. It's not yet on a par with top-tier destinations for retirees such as Malaysia or Thailand, and is clearly only for the adventurous type. It is a place to watch for future opportunities but that will be several years yet.

THE CHECKLIST

1. Cost of living: Cheap, cheap, cheap. You can upgrade to a high level for very little. Food cheap, restaurants and utilities and internet cheap. All good. Thumbs up.
2. Buying or renting: Rules apply for buying but still inexpensive. Renting a much better option. Thumbs up.
3. Health care: Developing. Local care is okay thanks in large measure to the French heritage. New Thai facilities being built. Good but only in Phnom Penh or Siem Reap. Thumbs only partly up.
4. Visas and immigration: Surprisingly easy, straightforward, and user-friendly process but beware the rules can change. Thumbs up for now.

part III

The Not-So-Fun Stuff
You Need to Know

chapter 8

A Guide to Taxes, RRSPs, and Other Financial Issues to Help You Maximize Your Money Overseas

L et's face it: no one likes talking about taxes.

In fact, I would rather shovel snow for the next three months than have to deal with them. But taxes—like brutal winters in Winnipeg—are a fact of life. It just has to be done. That's the bad news.

Here's the good news: there is a resource that will solve your tax issues quickly and easily. It's called your professional accountant or tax planner.

Seriously, why would you want to deal with this on your own? We didn't want to, and that is why we hired a superlative tax specialist to manage the details of this chapter for us.

Trust us, it's worth it. Planning for a carefree and blissful retirement shouldn't make you crazy. Of course, you must be keenly aware of the implications of leaving Canada on a full- or part-time basis. It requires careful planning and preparation. But as sure as we can be that the cost of living in Vancouver will keep going up before it goes down and that the Toronto Maple Leafs will not win the Stanley Cup (ever), you will definitely need professional advice.

Consider this chapter a primer on the key areas that you should cover with your expatriate tax advisor. The importance of using a professional who deals primarily with offshore tax issues can't be overstated. Our advisors, Wayne Bewick and Shalia Patel of Trowbridge Professional Corporation, applied their knowledge of the Canadian tax system as global expatriate tax advisors and were invaluable in making sure the guidance contained here was correct.

(And Wayne is a fellow Canadian to boot.)

So here we go. And be patient. It isn't like we are going to spring a pop quiz at the end. This is complicated stuff and no one expects you to get it the first time through.

Everyone's tax situation is different and depends on a variety of factors, like income, age, the nature of your investments, the geographic spread of your assets, and whether you keep a home in Canada. It is a long list but there are some general rules that apply and you need to be on top of all them if you are going to avoid a nasty surprise from our Canadian tax authorities down the road.

The last thing you need is for the CRA
to decide you really are a resident of Canada
due to material ties you have maintained, despite
leaving the country years ago, and charge
you back taxes on your global earnings.

In this chapter we deal primarily with establishing full-time non-residency in Canada. For those people who would consider a part-time move, the most important consideration is the number of days Canada allows you to be out of the country and still retain your home country benefits. This is generally pegged at 183 days but varies by province (Ontario and Newfoundland allow residents 212 days out of the country).

Therefore, you can leave the country for at least half the year, continue to pay Canadian taxes on *all* your income (worldwide), maintain your Canadian health care (although provincial health care coverage varies by province, it can be severely limited offshore). Supplemental travel insurance is a must for most provinces and a good idea for the rest.

As a "part-time resident," you need to be aware that although you are a continuing resident of Canada and enjoy the benefits of continuing Canadian residency, you may also inadvertently establish residency ties in the country you are spending the winter in. These situations have to be considered carefully and discussed with professionals prior to making the decision.

RESIDENCY

The most critical aspect to consider for your taxation status is whether you will be a resident or non-resident for tax purposes once you move overseas. You can either be a resident or a non-resident of Canada but never both, and residency requires both husband and wife to be of the same country status. But it is more a matter of fact and circumstances than it is applied law. There are no hard and fast rules, only guidelines. At the end of the day, the Canada Revenue Agency (CRA) will determine your residency status based largely on a set of suggested "ties to Canada" from a list that includes what they describe as major and minor ties. We will get to that list in a minute.

Simply put, taxes imposed on individuals are based on their status either as a resident or non-resident. Therefore, determining whether or not residency has ceased is important, as is the date of the change.

Unfortunately, no simple, clear-cut rule or definition exists for determining when an individual ceases residency; basically the CRA makes its judgment on a case-by-case basis. Not exactly Las Vegas but you get the idea.

*Tattoo "residency" on your forehead–
metaphorically speaking–because the tax
consequences of getting it wrong are really
important and can be really bad.*

The CRA considers the following factors when determining whether an individual remains a resident of Canada for tax purposes even though they may have gone abroad:

- Evidence of *intention* to permanently sever residential ties
- Residential ties to Canada versus residential ties elsewhere
- Regularity and length of visits to Canada

Evidence of Intention to Permanently Sever Residential Ties

Here is where the "ties to Canada" criteria come into play. First up, there must be a degree of permanence to the stay abroad. Are you in the country on a residency permit? Or are you just there on a short-term visitor visa? It is the intent that matters. It doesn't mean you have to purchase a home or condo in

Bali or Penang to convince the taxman you are a non-resident. An extended stay visa, a long-term rental agreement (at least a year), and the disposition or long-term rental of Canadian property can be considered strong evidence that your intent is to leave Canada, not just for an extended holiday or as a short-term tax exile.

These are important "major ties" that signal that your departure from Canada is *intended* to be long term. Slightly less important are "minor ties," such as maintaining Canadian bank accounts, credit cards, a driver's licence, and keeping a car or a local phone account. These secondary ties, in and of themselves, are not generally seen as non-residency deal breakers, but it is the addition of any of them to a continuing "major tie" that the taxman will consider in determining if your non-residency status is legit.

Residential Ties to Canada Versus Elsewhere

Some of the following steps indicate you have severed your ties to Canada:

- Spouse/common-law partner and dependants leave Canada—either with you or shortly thereafter
- Renting your home to an unrelated party on a long-term basis or selling it
- Long-term lease in the foreign country or home purchased in the foreign country
- Moving personal property out of Canada
- Notifying bankers, insurance company, or other financial institutions of your move
- Cancelling or minimizing credit cards
- Cancelling health coverage under the provincial health care plan

A short-term lease on your owned former family home, retention of an ongoing lease on a rental property, possession of a Canadian telephone number, or retaining a Canadian postal address or a driver's licence can jeopardize your claim that you have left Canada permanently.

Regularity and Length of Visits to Canada

An occasional family vacation or a business-related trip back to Canada would not affect your residency claim. However, if the return visits are regular and lengthy, it can be an indication that the individual has not developed stronger ties with the new country of residence. This may cause the CRA to find that the individual has retained links with Canada and is therefore a continuing resident.

Date Residency Ends

CRA's administrative policy as outlined in its manuals is that if you cease being a Canadian resident, the date your residency ends generally is the latest of these:

- The date you leave Canada
- The date you established residency in the foreign country
- The date your family leaves Canada

The actual date your residency ends is significant for a number of tax reasons, including certain dollar amounts such as various personal credits, that may be prorated based on the number of days you were resident in Canada that year.

There may be situations where you need to complete Form NR73, Determination of Residence Status (Leaving Canada). Your expat accountant can determine if it is necessary to do so.

Withholding Taxes while a Non-resident

If you thought you were done with the taxman once you sever residency ties, think again! Certain types of income paid or credited to non-residents continue to be subject to withholding tax at 25 per cent in Canada; however, the withholding rate is reduced under many foreign tax treaties Canada has entered into.

The most common types of income subject to withholding tax are these:

- Dividends
- Rental income
- Pension and retirement income
- Payments out of Registered Retirement Savings Plans (RRSP) and Registered Retirement Income Funds (RRIF)

It is important to notify banks, brokers, insurance companies, and other potential payers of your non-resident status. A written notice should be provided and specifically request that non-resident tax be withheld from payments, where applicable. Most interest income is not subject to withholding tax.

You may also be subject to withholding tax if you sell Canadian real estate while a non-resident.

Departing from Canada

As a person ceasing to be a resident of Canada, you are deemed to have disposed of your capital assets at their fair market value on the date Canadian residency is relinquished. An exemption to this deemed disposal rule exists for certain assets, including these:

- Canadian property, which generally is taxed in Canada on actual disposition
- Canadian business property and inventory
- Unexercised stock options
- Assets held in various types of pension plans such as RRSPs, company pension plans, and other pension rights

Also, individuals who were residents of Canada for five years or less during the preceding ten-year period are exempt from the deemed disposition rule with regard to properties they either owned at the time they first became Canadian residents or that they inherited while they were resident in Canada, so long as they own the property when their Canadian residency ends.

Any accrued gains or losses for the assets subject to the deemed disposition rule are reported on the individual's Canadian tax return for the year of departure, with half of any net gains added to the individual's taxable income and taxed at marginal rates on that tax return.

An election is available to postpone the payment of the Canadian tax on gains realized under the deemed disposition rule until the year the subject property is actually disposed of. In order to defer tax payments that would otherwise be payable on departure, adequate security in lieu of tax on any gains realized as a result of the deemed disposition of assets may be required to be posted. The CRA has discretion to determine what constitutes "adequate security." Generally, no security is required on the tax arising on the first $100,000 of deemed capital gains.

If Canadian residency is re-established, the departure tax can be reversed if the individual elects to do so, provided he or she still holds the subject assets and the value of those assets has not fallen below the gain accrued at the departure date.

REGISTERED RETIREMENT SAVINGS PLANS

Contributions to Registered Retirement Savings Plans (RRSP)

As long as individuals have unused contribution room available, they can contribute to their RRSP regardless of their residency status. However, while a non-resident, the individual may not have ongoing Canadian income, so the RRSP deduction will not apply and will not provide a tax benefit. If a contribution is made as a non-resident with the intention of carrying it forward, a tax return is required to report the contribution and unused carry-forward. Unused contributions can be carried forward indefinitely and deducted on a future Canadian return. There are situations when, as a non-resident, an individual may have Canadian income—for example, he or she may have Canadian-source employment income from the exercise of stock options that were unexercised at the time of departure. RRSP deductions can be claimed on such tax returns but only to the extent there is contribution room available.

There may be restrictions on how the money in your RRSP can be invested while you are a non-resident. Financial advisors or financial institutions are in the best position to provide guidance in this matter.

Withdrawals from RRSPs

Any amount can be withdrawn from an RRSP (or RRIF) as a non-resident; however, the amounts are subject to tax. The rate of tax applicable to the withdrawal depends on the individual's residency status at the time of the withdrawal:

- If the withdrawal is made while you are a resident in Canada, the withdrawals will have tax withheld at statutory fixed rates, but are ultimately taxed at normal marginal rates.
- If the withdrawal is made while you are a non-resident, the withdrawal is subject to a 25 per cent withholding tax. This rate may be reduced to 15 per cent by treaty if the withdrawal is in the form of an annuity. If the withdrawal from the RRSP occurs when you are in the new country of residence and the income is taxed in that country as well, you may be entitled to a foreign tax credit for Canadian withholding tax paid.

Home Buyer's Plan/Lifelong Learning Plan Amounts

If you have "borrowed" from your RRSP under the Home Buyer's Plan (HBP) or Lifelong Learning Plan (LLP), these loans must be repaid in full when you become a non-resident. The repayment must be made within sixty days of the date you cease to be a Canadian resident, otherwise any amounts you borrowed that you failed to repay will be included in the income reported in your part-year return.

TAX-FREE SAVINGS ACCOUNTS

The Tax-Free Savings Account (TFSA) was introduced in 2009 as a registered savings account that allows taxpayers to earn investment income tax-free inside the account. Although contributions to the account are not deductible for tax purposes, withdrawals of contributions and earnings from the account are not taxable.

Each year every Canadian resident 18 years of age and older is allocated and allowed to contribute a maximum amount to a TFSA ($5,500 for 2014, indexed for inflation).

Similar to RRSPs, unused contribution room can be carried forward to future years, and excess contributions would be subject to tax of 1 per cent per month, for each month that the excess remains in the plan.

If you become a non-resident, you can continue to maintain your existing TFSA, and you would not be taxed by Canada on any earnings in the account or on withdrawals. However, you are not permitted to make any contributions to a TFSA and you do not accrue any additional contribution room for a year in which you are a non-resident of Canada. In your year of departure from Canada, you may wish to make a contribution to your TFSA prior to leaving Canada if you have room available.

CANADA PENSION PLAN/ OLD AGE SECURITY

If the taxpayer is qualified to receive the social security benefits from Canada and is no longer resident in Canada, the pension and benefit payments could be subject to non-resident tax withholding. The withholding rate is 25 per cent unless reduced or exempted by the income tax treaty between Canada and the country of residence.

The non-resident tax will be withheld from the payments directly by Service Canada. Any income and tax withheld will be reported to the taxpayer on an NR4 tax information slip. It is important to ensure that you advise Service Canada as soon as you can that you are departing Canada.

Depending on your worldwide income, there is a possibility that you will be subject to the Old Age Security "clawback" if your income is too high and you may have to repay part or all of the Old Age Security pension. Depending on the country of residence, an Old Age Security Return of Income (OASRI) form may be required to be submitted before June 30 of the following year.

CANADIAN EMPLOYMENT AND SELF-EMPLOYMENT INCOME

Non-residents of Canada are generally subject to federal and provincial income taxes on employment income earned in Canada in the same manner—using the same rates and income bands—as Canadian residents. The key difference is that non-residents are generally not eligible for the personal tax credits, such as basic personal amount and spousal amount, against the tax payable. In addition, non-residents are subject to federal and provincial tax on income from carrying on a business in Canada. There could be income tax treaty exemptions from tax on both employment and self-employment income, however—that is something a tax professional specialized in expatriate tax can discuss. A non-resident must report the relevant income and any deductions and calculate the income tax on a non-resident tax return (Form T1NR).

The tax return must be filed on or before April 30 of the following year, except that the return for income from a business carried on in Canada must be filed by June 15 of the following year. The final payment of tax in all cases, however, is due April 30. Furthermore, a separate Quebec non-resident tax return must be filed with the Quebec Ministry of Revenue (by the same deadline: April 30) if the employment income or self-employment income was earned in Quebec. If insufficient tax is withheld from the relevant income at source, installments may have to be paid during the year.

CANADIAN WITHHOLDING TAX ON INVESTMENT INCOME

A federal 25 per cent withholding tax applies to investment income, including certain interest, royalties, pension income, rents, and dividends, when such income is paid from a Canadian source to a non-resident. The 25 per cent withholding tax, which is deducted at source, may be reduced under an income tax treaty to rates ranging from 0 per cent to 15 per cent. Canadian withholding tax does not apply to interest (except for "participating debt interest") paid to non-residents. The payer is required to issue a non-resident tax slip with the correct withholding.

A reduction in the amount of withholding (possibly to 0 per cent) is also available to non-residents for rental income. This is discussed in detail below under "Renting out Your Canadian Home."

As indicated previously, depending on the country of residence, the income may be subject to tax in that country and, if so, the individual may be eligible for a foreign tax credit for the tax withheld in Canada.

SPECIAL RETURNS

A non-resident may elect to file a Canadian income tax return in respect of certain other types of Canadian income, such as pension benefits, retiring allowances, and/or other specified benefits. Such an election is beneficial only when the amount of tax imposed on the income at graduated rates is less than the withholding tax that would otherwise be imposed. There are stringent rules and deadlines for the filing of these returns.

SALE OF CANADIAN HOME (PRINCIPAL RESIDENCE)

Many people moving to a foreign country have a home that served as their principal residence in Canada. If that principal residence is sold by a resident of Canada, any capital gain arising from the sale of it is exempt from capital gains tax so long as two conditions are met:

- The individual has been a Canadian resident for the entire period the home was owned, and
- The home was always the principal residence

Special rules apply to ensure a family designates only one principal residence for tax purposes at any given time.

Selling Your Home while a Non-resident

If the home is sold after ceasing residence in Canada, a portion of the gain may be subject to tax. The following formula is used to determine the exempt portion of the gain:

The number of years you were a resident of Canada and the property was your principal residence (not rented out) plus one grace year

Therefore, if a taxpayer ceases Canadian residency at any time in year X, for the entire gain to be exempt, the sale must happen no later than year X+1 (within one year of the date of ceasing residency). For the purposes of this formula, a part year will count as a grace year. In our case, we sold our house to our tenants after renting it to them for four years and, as non-residents, had to pay capital gains tax. Since we had owned the house for ten years, the formula reduced our tax on the gain to 17.5 per cent.

(By the way, how are you holding up? Eyes glazed over yet? Time for a break? Hang in there! We're almost home.)

Also factored in were deductions for real estate commissions, legal fees, transfer taxes (if paid by the seller), certain fixing-up expenses, and fees for the preparation of a compliance application (for the sale of a Canadian property by a non-resident of Canada). Rather than face withholding of 25 per cent of gross proceeds (point one below), we filed to have it apply to only 25 per cent of the gain (point two below).

Here is a nice, clean example of a typical calculation:

You owned your house for nine years before moving to another country and then rented it out for the next six years before selling it. While your total ownership was fifteen years, you are credited with just the nine years you owned and occupied it plus the one-year grace period for a total of ten years. Say your gain on the house was $90,000. Since CRA recognizes ten years out of the fifteen, two-thirds of your gain would be tax exempt less deductions. Easy, eh?

Here is a proper taxman's explanation of the two approaches. Clearly, the second is the most viable for the majority of people.

1. Certification and withholding procedures apply. Under the certification procedure, the purchaser of the property must withhold 25 per cent of the gross proceeds and remit it to Canada Revenue Agency.
2. Under an alternative certification and withholding method, the individual himself/herself can apply to CRA

to have the withholding tax reduced to 25 per cent of the taxable gain. To qualify under this alternative method, the application must be made no later than ten days after the disposition (sale of your house). In order to take advantage of this method, it is a good idea to contact tax professionals for assistance.

If you obtain a clearance certificate from CRA, you will be required to file a non-resident tax return to report the disposition and receive a refund of any tax withheld.

Renting out Your Canadian Home

As mentioned earlier, there are tax consequences related to renting your Canadian home or other real estate situated in Canada. The two issues are these:

1. The tax consequences of earning Canadian rental income while a non-resident (for both your previous principal residence and other real estate) and in case of your Canadian home
2. The capital gains issues that arise when your principal residence is converted to rental use

Tax Consequences of Earning Rental Income while Non-resident

The gross rental income received from rental property located in Canada (irrespective of whether this was the former principal residence or some other property) is normally subject to withholding tax at a rate of 25 per cent. The tenant or an agent (the agent must be a resident of Canada) acting on the taxpayer's behalf must withhold and remit the tax to CRA by the fifteenth day of the month following the month in which the rent was paid (as an example, withholding tax for rental income received in January must be remitted to the CRA by the fifteenth day of February). If tax is not withheld and remitted, CRA will charge compound daily interest and may also charge a penalty.

The agent must provide the taxpayer and any other owner with an information slip (NR4 "Statement of Amounts Paid or Credited to Non-residents of Canada") showing the gross amount of rental income paid or credited during the year. The Canadian agent is also required to file an NR4 return with CRA by March 30 of the year after the year in which rental income was received.

If the appropriate withholding tax on the gross rental income is remitted, there is no need to file a Canadian tax return to report the rental income.

Deemed Disposition on Change-of-Use

Generally, when a principal residence is converted to a rental property, there is a deemed disposition at fair market value on the date of conversion. (This is true regardless of whether you are resident or non-resident when the conversion occurs.) The gain resulting from the deemed disposition may be entirely or partially exempt under the principal residence exemption as described earlier (under sale of property).

Also, as it is only a deemed disposition (as opposed to an actual one), it is deemed that you have acquired the rental property at the same value on the same date. (Similarly, there would be a deemed disposition of the rental property if you reoccupy the home, and at that point you could have a capital gain, recapture of capital cost allowance [CCA], or a terminal loss). There is a special election available enabling you to elect no change-in-use has occurred for your principal residence. As with all elections, you are required to adhere to some stringent rules.

Option to Claim Rental Expenses

It is possible to pay tax only on the net Canadian-source rental income instead of on the gross amount by filing a "Non-resident Rental Tax Return." Net rental income is determined by taking gross rental income less expenses incurred to earn the income, such as property tax, capital cost allowance (CCA, or tax depreciation), mortgage interest, the cost of repairs, et cetera. The tax due on the net rental income is calculated based on normal personal tax rates. A two-year time limit applies (two years from the end of the tax year in which rental income was earned).

If the tax withheld by the Canadian agent was more than the amount of tax payable as calculated on the non-resident rental return, CRA will refund the difference to the taxpayer.

Electing to Have Tax Withheld on Net Rental Income

If the individual decides it is more advantageous to file a non-resident rental return, he or she can elect to have the Canadian agent withhold and remit tax based on the net rental income (instead of gross income). To make this election, a request has to be sent to the CRA prior to the end of the previous tax year (or prior to beginning to rent the property). This request has to be made every year that the property is owned by you as a non-resident and rented. Only upon CRA's written approval can the agent withhold (and remit) tax from the net monthly rental income instead of the gross.

If withholding tax is not remitted to the CRA, there will be an interest charge, and the taxpayer and/or the agent may also be liable for a penalty.

We all have a certain degree of fear of the taxman. The process of leaving Canada and giving up residency may appear daunting but, in fact, it is pretty straightforward. It requires the assistance of a professional who can manage the necessary paperwork, the required declarations, et cetera. Our own departure was no hardship at all. Declaring the rental income from our Canadian house for taxes and, years later, calculating capital gains tax over and above its declared value when we sold the house was all easily done. Through the years we have managed our RRSPs with hardly any difficulty, although there are some investment restrictions that apply to non-residents, and, of course, with no Canadian-sourced income we could no longer contribute to them. In hindsight we broke many of the "minor tie" rules when we declared non-residency. We kept a car in storage and retained bank accounts, credit cards, driver's licences, et cetera, for many years. However, we did sell our primary Canadian residence and have had a series of offshore employment passes, long-term visas, and rental agreements that our advisors tell us are sufficient evidence to indicate we left the country with no intention of returning for a very long time, if ever.

Now, as we are approaching pension age, we want to be clear on double taxation issues and how they may apply to us. Fortunately, Thailand, Vietnam, and Indonesia all have tax treaties with Canada that protect non-residents from double taxation on government or private pensions or RRSP income. Malaysia also has a treaty but it is currently under review to be upgraded. Cambodia does not have a tax treaty with Canada and likely won't for years to come.

Phew. That's it. You made it! I don't know about you, but right now I could go for one of those delicious local dollar beers ... oh right. Well, for you it might be five or six bucks.

The important thing is this: there are highly trained professionals like Wayne and Shalia out there who will be more than happy to guide you through the fog and deep snow. Remember, it's nothing but sunshine and warm tropical breezes at this end!

Tips and Traps: Taxation

1. The importance of using a professional advisor knowledgeable about expatriate tax issues cannot be overstated.
2. The most important factor to consider is the issue of maintaining your Canadian residency or declaring non-residence. The latter event triggers important actions to be taken.
3. Be aware that, even if you maintain Canadian residency and leave the country for the maximum allowable 183 days a year, your provincial heath care coverage may not provide adequate coverage offshore. The amount of coverage varies by province but, as a rule, supplemental travel insurance is a must.
4. Declared non-residents of Canada pay tax only on income derived in Canada. The inverse is true in the United States, where their tax follows them wherever they go in the world.
5. Pay particular attention to the documentation CRA requires on leaving the country for any extended period. It is just as important to Canadians to document their intentions whether it is a six-month sabbatical or a long-term/permanent departure.

chapter 9

It's All About
Preserving and Protecting
Your Biggest Asset:
Your Health

C hoosing your health insurance coverage is one of the most important decisions you face when you decide to relocate overseas either full time or for part of the year.

And this choice presents a real dilemma. There are two extremes: (1) Full international health insurance is very expensive, but (2) lack of health insurance can be catastrophic.

Luckily there are middle paths that can be taken. As a general rule, if you can afford full health coverage, take it out. It is worth it for peace of mind.

The people we spoke to in the research for this book had very firm—and very different—views on health insurance. The views ranged from the blissfully unconcerned—"I can't afford it, so I don't worry about it"—to the cynical—"They never pay up. You can be sure of one thing: if you are over 60 anything that goes wrong with you will be considered a pre-existing condition." Included too was the somewhat impractical—"I will just go back to Canada if I get really sick or need an operation"—or the (frankly) terrifying—"It is not worth having it. My friend died while the insurer argued with the doctor about whether she needed to be medically evacuated."

At least half the people we interviewed had no health insurance at all. To be honest, that was a real shock to us. Of the remainder, a few had international health insurance policies but most relied on travel insurance policies for peace of mind. Remember the Danish Arctic explorer Roald Amundsen? He said that adventure was the result of bad planning. We agree. Taking a risk on an unfamiliar item on a menu is what life is all about; gambling with your health is just crazy.

Let us look at the options. There are essentially three broad categories, in descending order of expense:

1. An international health insurance policy
2. A travel insurance policy
3. No insurance at all, usually with the intention of returning to Canada and relying on provincial or territorial health insurance and, in some cases, private Canadian health insurance coverage

There is no guarantee that your provincial medical plan will cover you out of the country whether you are gone weeks or months. At best, it varies by province but travel insurance will cover you, and usually it includes costly items like medical evacuation.

NO INSURANCE

This is, of course, the riskiest option. When you choose this option you are, perhaps unconsciously, making a number of assumptions, such as these:

- You have enough funds to cover occasional visits to the local doctor for temporary illnesses.
- If you suffer in the future from a chronic illness, you will return to Canada and be treated under your provincial or territorial health plan and/or your Canadian private insurance.
- If you have a serious accident while overseas, you can afford care in local hospitals and the local hospitals are capable of providing adequate care. Alternatively, you have enough savings to cover the cost of an emergency medical evacuation.

If you are prepared to accept these assumptions, you need to be aware of a few facts.

The first relates to your provincial or territorial health insurance. If you have given up Canadian residency, there is not much chance (with a few exceptions) that your medical and hospital treatments will be covered by provincial or territorial health insurance during return visits to Canada. The bigger surprise is that provincial or territorial health insurance varies by province and territory and, in the worst cases, will provide very little coverage even if you maintain Canadian residency and are out of the country for just days, let alone weeks or months.

Provincial or territorial health insurance, Canada's health care system, is principally designed to serve Canadians *living in* Canada.

The Canada Health Act defines insured persons as residents of a province. The Act further defines a resident this way:

> A person lawfully entitled to be or to remain in Canada
> who makes his home and is ordinarily present in the
> province, but does not include a tourist, a transient or
> a visitor to the province.

Therefore, residence in a province or territory is the basic requirement for provincial or territorial health insurance coverage. Each province and territory is responsible for determining its own minimum residence requirements with regard to an individual's eligibility for benefits under its health insurance plan. The Canada Health Act gives no guidance on such residence requirements beyond limiting waiting periods to establish eligibility for and entitlement to insured health services to three months. Most provinces and territories also require residents to be physically present 183 days annually and no more than 183 days out of the country, and residents must provide evidence of their intent to return to the province.

If you will be away for longer than that, you can apply for continuous health insurance eligibility. This means that you want to keep your health insurance benefits, even though you will be out of the country for more than 183 days. Your provincial or territorial health insurance may cover you for a longer period of time if you are out of the country because you are

- Studying
- Working
- Vacationing
- Doing missionary work

To apply for continuous health insurance eligibility, you might need to show documents explaining why you will be absent.

When you are outside the country, coverage is required to be at home-province or territory rates. As a result, health care services received abroad may not be fully covered by a provincial or territorial health insurance plan. For that reason, it is highly recommended that you purchase supplemental private insurance before leaving Canada, to ensure adequate coverage.

So it is *possible* to take the risky route on health insurance. But it can devastate your savings if you have a medical emergency and need to be medically evacuated to another country. And if you contract a chronic disease, such as cancer, you will most likely be forced to return to Canada. Long periods of treatment involving chemotherapy and radiotherapy don't come cheap, even in the low-cost-of-living countries in Asia.

TRAVEL INSURANCE POLICIES

Travel insurance policies can be as low as $700 a year if you include a deductible of at least $100 on every claim. This means that you pay the first $100 of every eligible bill and the insurance company picks up the rest. Any claim for pre-existing medical conditions are excluded from the standard policy, although it is possible to negotiate with the insurer to include certain pre-existing conditions for an additional fee.

Most travel insurance policies make it clear that the medical coverage is only for "unexpected sudden illnesses or serious conditions." Remember, travel insurance includes everything from lost baggage to stolen property and flight interruptions. The emergency medical coverage is only one part of the policy. But the great attraction of travel insurance policies for expatriate

Canadians in Asia is that they generally include overseas evacuation costs. This coverage looks generous. Standard policies boast that they will cover medical, dental, and evacuation costs of up to $300,000. Surely that would cover the most dire emergency? Well, it might. But make sure you read the fine print in the policy documents. The product disclosure statement is the document that must be gone through with a fine-tooth comb.

These are the traps to keep an eye on:

- Most global policies won't cover applicants over 74 years of age unless they submit to a medical appraisal questionnaire first. The largest Canadian travel insurer requires a medical questionnaire be submitted by every applicant over 55. This can range from answering a set of questions online, right through to a full physical examination signed off by a medical practitioner if you are over 70.
- Travel insurance is usually for a maximum of twelve months and renewable for a further twelve months. Big reputable insurers, like Bupa, for example, will not renew policies after twenty-four months. And there is a trap in the renewal provisions. If you contracted an illness during the first twelve months of the policy, it is considered to be a pre-existing medical condition and therefore excluded, in many cases, from the coverage in the second year. This is the opposite of usual private health insurance where only pre-existing medical conditions that exist at the time you first take out the policy fall under the exclusions.
- It is worth having a close look at the definition of "pre-existing medical conditions." Some policies will have a list of conditions that are automatically pre-approved, including asthma, high cholesterol, and high blood pressure. The kicker is that you must declare these

conditions when you apply for the policy. If you don't, they could be excluded from coverage.

When an insurer excludes a pre-existing medical condition, it will also exclude *any consequences of the condition*. We have seen policies that use the expression "direct or indirect consequences." What the heck does that mean? Essentially, it means run like hell. Now, we don't want to get into trouble with insurance companies. What we want to do is make sure you know what the rules are before you buy. The point is, the interpretation can be very broad.

For example, if your travel insurance policy excluded high blood pressure as a pre-existing condition, it would not only exclude the associated medicine but also any selected subsequent conditions such as a heart attack or angina. HealthCare International defines a pre-existing condition as "an illness, injury or related medical condition for which within the last five years you have experienced symptoms, received treatment, medication, advice or investigation."

That is pretty broad.

> Some insurance plans will not cover you
> at all for chronic illnesses such as cancer.
> Others provide 100 per cent coverage for
> things such as cancer or heart problems, even
> in their standard plans. Shop around.

MEDICAL EVACUATION

This is the big-ticket item that many expatriates fear most. For some, it is one of the two main reasons that they take out travel insurance, the other being on-ground hospital treatment in the event of a medical emergency.

Once again, it is important to scrutinize the fine print in the product disclosure statement.

Most policies will cover medical evacuation costs only if the insurance company's doctor agrees with the treating doctor that you need to be moved and if the insurance company organizes the transportation.

It is often stated that travel must be at the same fare class as originally selected by you. So if you have booked an economy return flight, the insurance company will fly you back economy unless the insurer's doctor agrees otherwise on the basis of a written recommendation by your attending physician.

Some policies also state that the insurer will not cover the cost of a full return ticket to Canada if you have not already booked and paid for it before the company returns you to Canada. In other words, you must have a return ticket already, and if you don't, then the ordinary cost of a flight back to Canada will be deducted from your claim. You can see there is a lot of room for discussion between the insurance company, yourself, and the treating doctor before a medical evacuation takes place.

Globally based medical evacuation companies such as Global Rescue and International IOS have policies specifically for medical evacuation, in some cases to your home country, in others to a preferred "suitable" medical facility, for very reasonable rates up to 75 years of age. By "reasonable" I mean as little as $550 a year, depending on circumstances. Given the horrendous cost of evacuation to the uninsured, this is a worthwhile expenditure, depending, of course, on the nature of your risk.

INTERNATIONAL HEALTH INSURANCE

This is the gold-plated option for health coverage. It doesn't come cheap. It can cost over $15,000 a year per person or as little as $2,000, depending on the level of coverage chosen, the size of the deductible, and the level of co-payment. An example of co-payment would be that you pay the first $100 of each claim and 20 per cent of the amount in excess of $100, in order to reduce your premiums.

The two key pieces of advice for anyone seeking to purchase international health coverage is to shop around and read the fine print of the product disclosure statements. My own international coverage from London took a giant leap when I turned 64. I refused to give in and found another company, just as reputable, in Hong Kong and my premium was reduced from $9,000 a year to just under $5,000. It is worth taking the time to shop around.

The big Canadian health insurers, such as Manulife or Sun Life, all offer international products. You may feel more comfortable dealing with a Canadian insurer that has been efficient—and has paid up promptly without issue—in the past. But remember that there is a big international market out there for expatriate health insurance and it is very competitive. Internet sites, such as Medibroker, provide brokering services and comparisons of over thirty different health insurers. Big U.K.-based companies like HealthCare International and Bupa carry a comprehensive range of health insurance packages.

Choosing the cheapest option may not be the best idea. You need an insurer with a good reputation and one that is recognized by the major hospitals and quality medical practitioners in your country of residence. Check out the hospital that you are most likely to use and ask them which insurers they accept.

Most health insurers provide a basic plan plus a number of add-on options to choose from. Or they may provide different levels of coverage—for example, bronze, gold, and platinum.

Some plans will not cover you at all for chronic illnesses, such as cancer. Others provide 100 per cent coverage for cancer treatment even in their standard plans. You can also add coverage for some pre-existing conditions. Check carefully how the insurer defines pre-existing condition and scrutinize the policy for the "fine print" about renewals. For instance, will the insurer consider your pre-existing conditions to be only those that existed when you first took out the policy or is there a new test every time you renew? Does the policy cover you for treatment and/or continuous coverage back in Canada? Does the policy allow you to renew over the age of 70? Do premiums go up every year with age?

It is important that the insurers have twenty-four-hour seven-day-a-week contact numbers and foreign language skills if possible. If your condition is serious and requires a big upfront payment, can they help you deal with that by wire-transferring funds if your credit cards are maxed out?

Age is a big factor when it comes to premiums. That seems obvious, right? But what might not be so obvious is the exponential jump in premiums based on one year. As I said, when I turned 64 my premiums *doubled*. Talk about sticker shock! Anyway, even though you may be in the great shape at 67, that insurer is looking at a number and an attached risk evaluation. Our advice is, be smart and ask questions. Get the answers you want before you sign on the dotted line.

Your health is the single most important factor in ensuring that you enjoy your new life in your country of choice. Buy the best insurance coverage you can afford, but absolutely shop around before you purchase. In fact, consider using a broker to search out the policy that suits you best, and, above all, make sure you read the fine print in the product disclosure statement. Look, it's true: insurance is boring. But it is incredibly important, and the good part is that the most boring bits can be easily researched here at home. Be patient and do your homework. Retiring overseas is all about the happy and unexpected surprises, not the shocks.

Tips and Traps: Health Insurance

1. If you can afford and are eligible for full international health coverage, take it. It is worth it for peace of mind.
2. The cost of an uninsured emergency medical evacuation from Asia to a Western country (not necessarily Canada) or a "preferred" facility (Singapore) can be upwards of $40,000. The insurance cost is actually quite reasonable.
3. Travel insurance policies can be used as a stop-gap for health coverage but they are principally intended for emergencies. Read the fine print.
4. Tell the truth to your insurer about any pre-existing illnesses. Failure to do this can lead to a denial of claims.
5. International health insurance can be expensive, but there are a number of different levels of coverage from a standard to a gold policy and prices vary widely.
6. Shop around. International health insurance is a very competitive market.

➡

7. Check if your proposed insurance company is recognized by major health care providers in your new country of residence.

8. Provincial or territorial health insurance needs to be supplemented by a travel insurance policy. Your coverage back home is principally a health system for Canadians who live in Canada, not abroad.

9. Non-residents of Canada are not entitled to use provincial health insurance on visits home. And it doesn't matter if you are still paying taxes in Canada.

10. Once you have lived outside Canada for more than five years there is no flexibility—you are not entitled to provincial health insurance on visits home in any circumstance.

chapter 10

Everything You Need to Know About Visas

V isas are almost as boring as talking about taxes. In fact, visas are a lot like snowflakes (and we all know about snow!): each one is unique. Actually, that is an exaggeration. It is true that visas come in a lot of shapes and sizes. But the good news is that there is a ton of resources at your fingertips to help you navigate the rough waters.

What we have done here is simply summarize the visa requirement highlights for each country. It should be pretty easy to find the one that is right for you. And like we said, help is available to anyone who needs it (including our own Planet Boomer website!).

BALI VISA

Visas do not present a problem for those wishing to spend extended periods in Bali.

Canadian tourists can obtain a tourist visa on arrival. That is, at the airport when you land in Bali or Jakarta. This is a thirty-day single-entry visa, extendable to sixty days in-country, and costs $30 for each thirty-day term.

There are several types of visas that cover a longer period of stay in Indonesia. These are business visas, employment visas, and retirement visas. We will focus on the retirement visas for the purposes of this book.

Full details are listed below but there are a few general points to note for those who are close to retirement, or at retirement age, and do not wish to work in Indonesia. The retirement or renewable-stay visa is available to those over 55 years of age who can prove they have an income of at least $20,000 a year. Applicants must also show proof of health insurance in either their own country or Indonesia. They must agree to employ an Indonesian maid, not to work or undertake business activities, and show proof of accommodation that is either rented for at least $580 a month or purchased for at least $40,600. The visas are for one year but can be renewed in-country up to a maximum of five years. After five years, it is possible to apply for a permanent-stay visa or KITAP (permanent-stay permit).

Applying for a Retirement Visa

If you are 55 years of age or older, renewable-stay permits (or retirement visas) of one year's duration can be obtained for Indonesia.

This retirement visa requires the following:

- Applicant must be 55 years of age or older
- An application form completed in duplicate (this form is available from the Republic of Indonesia website www.embassyofindonesia.org)

- Applicant's passport with at least eighteen months' duration with a minimum of three blank pages
- Photocopy of all passport pages to be submitted along with passport photograph—ten 1.5 in. by 2.4 in. (4 cm by 6 cm) photographs, four 1.25 in. by 1.5 in. (3 cm by 4 cm) photographs, and four .75 in. by 1.25 in. (2 cm by 3 cm) photographs
- An applicant whose spouse wishes to apply for a retirement visa as well must supply a copy of the marriage licence
- A flight itinerary
- A curriculum vitae
- A bank statement or pension fund showing income of $1,700 a month or $20,400 a year
- Proof of health insurance, life insurance, and third-party personal liability insurance in country of origin or Indonesia
- A statement showing cost of accommodation
- Minimum purchase price of house or apartment of $40,600
- Minimum rental cost of $580 a month for Jakarta, Bandung, and Bali; $350 a month in other cities in Java, Batam, and Medan; $230 a month in other cities; copy of a lease or a letter from your landlord indicating you have a pending lease agreement
- A statement proving there is or will be employment of an Indonesian maid
- A statement agreeing not to engage in business activities or work

The maximum stay on the retirement visa is one year and this can be renewed five times, meaning a maximum stay of five years.

You can enter the country on a visit-on-arrival (VOA) visa and after a month apply for a longer-term (limited stay) permit.

The visa fee is $190, at time of writing.

If you use an agent, which does in fact make life a lot easier, the fees range from $465 to $650.

Permanent-stay Permit

After extending the visa five times (for a five-year stay), foreign retirees can apply for a permanent-stay visa or KITAP (Indonesian acronym for the permanent-stay permit) through the Foreign Tourist Bureau.

After you obtain a KITAP, citizenship or naturalization can be sought in a process over a year but certain qualifications need to be met by the retiree.

It is also easiest to use an Indonesian immigration agent to obtain a permanent-stay visa.

Business Visa

There are two types of business visas for people visiting Indonesia for normal business activities:

- A single-entry sixty-day visa
- A multiple-entry twelve-month visa

The visa applicant's business counterpart or an agent in Indonesia should apply in Indonesia on behalf of the applicant for a letter of approval from the Immigration Office of Indonesia.

Once the applicant has this letter of approval, he or she can then apply for a business visa.

The following documents are required for a business visa:

- A passport with a minimum validity of six months from the proposed date of entry into Indonesia
- A fully completed visa application form
- One passport-sized colour photograph
- Evidence that the applicant has sufficient funds to cover the cost of applicant's intended stay in Indonesia (e.g., a bank statement)

For the relevant business, the following are also required:

- Two supporting letters, one each from the applicant's company and the sponsor/counterpart in Indonesia, setting out the reason and duration of the proposed visit, and responsibility for incurred costs
- Copy of written approval from the Immigration Office in Jakarta, Indonesia, if the duration of business is to exceed sixty days

Employment Visa

Locally know as KITAS, employment visas are for foreign nationals who want to work in Indonesia.

An employment visa requires sponsorship by an Indonesian registered company. Just recently the government announced that KITAS visas would only be for six months and not for twelve anymore. Since it can take up to four months just to get the damn visa, this is hardly forward-thinking on the part of Indonesia. For the required documents, see the website www.visabali.com/employment-visas.php.

THAILAND VISA

Retirement visas are readily available in Thailand and full details are below. But first, a few general points.

You must be over 50 years old and have proof from your bank that you have either a bank balance of at least $28,000 or a monthly income of at least about $2,200. It is also possible to meet the test with a combination of bank balance plus income if your monthly income is less than $2,200.

You must also provide a police report from Canadian police. (These can take a while but are easily obtained from your local police station.) In addition, you must have a medical check to prove that you do not have a "prohibited disease."

The retirement visa is valid for twelve months and can be extended in-country. It is a multiple-entry visa but there is a requirement to report to immigration officials once every ninety days.

The visa application processing fee is $210.

How to Obtain a Retirement Visa in Thailand

The requirements for a retirement visa (also known as an OA visa) in Thailand are as follows:

- A passport with validity not less than eighteen months
- A copy of the entire passport—each page must be copied and signed
- Four completed and signed visa application forms—Form A—with one photo (1.25 in. by 1.75 in./3.5 cm by 4.5 cm) taken within the last six months, without wearing glasses or headgear (photocopy not accepted), attached to each of the four application forms
- A completed Personal Data Form (which can be downloaded from the Thai embassy in Ottawa [www. thaiembassy.ca] or obtained from consulate offices in Toronto, Vancouver, Edmonton, and Montreal)

- A copy of a bank statement showing a deposit of no less than $28,000, or an income statement (an original copy) with a monthly salary of no less than $2,200, or a deposit account plus monthly income of no less $28,000 a year
- An original copy of a letter from a bank or financial institution, stamped and signed by a bank officer, confirming sufficient funds
- A police name-check certificate issued no longer than three months prior to submitting the application
- A medical certificate indicating that the applicant has no prohibitive diseases as indicated in the Ministerial Regulation No. 14 (B.E. 2535), issued no longer than three months prior to submitting the application
- If the applicant's spouse does not qualify for a retirement visa in Thailand, a marriage certificate must be produced (the spouse will be considered for a non-immigrant visa category O)

Applicants may submit an application at the Royal Thai embassy or Royal Thai Consulate-General in their home or residence country or at the Office of the Immigration Bureau in Thailand located on Soi Suan Plu, South Sathorn Road, Sathorn District, Bangkok 10120. Tel 0-2287-4948 (direct) or 0-2287-3101-10, ext. 2236.

Important Visa Note

When you have prepared all the original documents as required above, you must then make three copies of each document. (Photos and signatures must not be photocopied.)

After you have made copies of all the documents, you must separate the documents into four sets. Within these sets, arrange the documents in the order given above. All together you will have one set of the original documents and three sets of copies.

After the four sets of documents have been prepared, you must take them to a notary public to bind and notarize each set of documents (the documents must be collated and bound only by the notary public).

Bringing Your Household Items to Thailand

You will be given six months from your entry to Thailand to bring in your household items from your country. If your permit grants you to stay for a year, these items will not be taxed. Otherwise, they will be taxed at a rate of 20 per cent for import duty and 7 per cent for value-added tax.

However, the deadline can be flexible. If you expect your items to arrive past the six-month deadline, you may inform the customs department two months before the deadline to request an extension. But this is not applicable on shipments arriving in some ports, especially Bangkok.

Obtaining a Re-entry Permit

Most people misunderstand the concepts of "extension of stay" and "re-entry permit." These are two distinct categories. You need both during your stay.

The extension of stay is simply the controlling date of arrival and departure. Everything else is dependent on this. It is all invalidated when your extension of stay expires. However, leaving Thailand without a re-entry permit also automatically invalidates your extension of stay, so you need to know the following:

- Extension of stay can be requested at the Office of Immigration Bureau (see details above)

- At the end of the twelve-month stay, if you wish to extend your stay you can submit a request for the extended period of stay at the Immigration Bureau along with evidence of money transfer, or a deposit account in Thailand, or an income statement proving that you have $28,000 on account, or an income statement with a deposit account that adds up to no less than $28,000 a year
- If your spouse wishes to extend his or her stay as well, a marriage certificate has to be produced

The granting of a one-year extension of stay is at the discretion of the immigration officer as long as the individual meets the above requirements.

Reporting Your Stay Every Ninety Days and Visa Expiration

You are required to report to the Immigration Police every ninety days if you are on a long-term extension of stay. Individuals holding a multiple-entry visa will simply depart Thailand and renew their extension of stay after each ninety-day entry.

If you cannot obtain your extension inside Thailand, you will have to get a new non-immigrant visa from a Thai embassy or consulate abroad.

Restrictions on Retirement Visa

The retirement visa, once approved, allows you to stay in Thailand for one year. You are not allowed to have employment while on this type of visa.

Retirement visa holders are also restricted from owning houses or land in Thailand. However, all visitors to Thailand, including tourists with no long-term visa, are able to purchase condominiums, apartments, and other residences that do not include the purchase of Thai national land.

MALAYSIA VISA

Malaysia is the most retiree-friendly country in Asia. The Malaysia My Second Home (MM2H) program offers non-Malaysians a ten-year renewable multiple-entry visa. This is very attractive to retirees. It gives certainty of tenure. It provides a streamlined application process. And it is tax friendly—all non-Malaysian income is tax-free for MM2H visa holders.

Just a few general pointers before we get into the details of the program. There are different rules for the under-50s and the 50-plus. The income and asset test for applicants is relatively high. You will need proof of liquid assets (cash on deposit) of at least $116,000 and an income of at least $3,300 a month if you are 50 or older. (It is slightly higher for the under-50s.) This benchmark will be lowered if you buy property in Malaysia. You will also need proof of health insurance coverage in Malaysia (although this can be waived if you can show that an insurance company has denied your application on the basis of age). A police report and a health check are also required.

So far, some 23,000 people have been approved, according to the Malaysian government.

The program is primarily attracting people who wish to retire in Malaysia or spend extended periods there.

The government website www.mm2h.gov.my/index.php/en/ provides all the required documents and application forms, and the following website outlines clearly the step-by-step process: www.mm2h.gov.my/index.php/en/apply-now/where-to-apply/steps-to-apply.

Applicants have the option of using an approved MM2H agent or submitting their application directly. Using an agent makes the process a lot easier and avoids the need to place a cash security bond (the agent will sponsor you). But this, of course, involves paying the agent their fee.

All agents have to be approved by the Ministry of Tourism. These can be identified by the initials (MM2H) in their company name. The Malaysian government sets the maximum fee that an agent can charge an applicant at $3,300.

The MM2H Application

Applications can be submitted while you are in Malaysia or can be submitted from overseas.

Once the committee reviews the documents (original submission) and approves the application, a letter of "conditional approval" is issued. The applicant then has six months to complete the remaining conditions (obtain medical insurance, complete the medical examination, and open the fixed deposit account) and collect the visa.

Document Requirements

The following documents are required to complete the application process, some at the time of original submission and others after receiving the letter of conditional approval:

- Covering letter: this should state the names of all people who are applying with you, how you will support yourself in Malaysia, and which financial criteria you wish to use (see below)
- Three copies of IM.12 Social Visit Pass (You can download this form and others from www.mm2h.com/mm2h-application-forms.php.)

- One copy of the Application Form MM2H
- Four passport-sized photographs of the applicant; if accompanied by a spouse, you also need four photos of your spouse
- Certified true copies of all pages of passport or other travel document of applicant (and spouse if relevant); all certified true copies of documents must be counter-signed by an embassy, high commission, justice of the peace, commissioner for oaths, solicitor, lawyer, or notary public.
- Certified true copy of every page of previous passport if your current passport is less than one year old (only the page with personal particulars needs to be certified)
- Certified true copy of marriage certificate if accompanied by spouse
- Certified true copy of children's birth certificates if accompanied by children
- A current resumé outlining employment history of primary applicant
- Evidence of financial assets
- Evidence of regular monthly income
- Medical report of applicant: Form RB1; this can be a self-declaration initially but after the conditional approval letter is issued, it must be signed off by a doctor in Malaysia
- Letter of good conduct by a government agency where you currently live (if you have lived there several years) or your home country (usually the police department)
- Authorization letter from applicant to Malaysia My Second Home Centre, which allows them to verify

the financial documents with the relevant financial institutions
- Evidence of purchasing property in Malaysia for more than $330,000 if requesting approval to make lower fixed deposit

Once the application is approved, you will be issued a conditional approval letter. This can be presented to any bank in Malaysia to open an account.

Visa Collection on Conditional Approval

After receiving the letter of conditional approval, the following documents must be submitted when collecting the visa:

- Evidence of placing the fixed deposit—if applying under this criterion
- Copy of Malaysian or global medical insurance
- Copy of locally sourced medical examination report
- A letter of good conduct from your home police department

All applications for people who want to live in West (peninsular) Malaysia are submitted to the My Second Home Centre in the Ministry of Tourism, which has information about the program.

Applications to live in Sabah or Sarawak have to be submitted to the respective state immigration offices. Agents can assist with application for peninsular Malaysia and Sabah. If you wish to live in Sarawak, you will have to contact the authorities in that state as they do not permit agents to assist with submissions of applications.

Malaysia My Second Home Centre
Ministry of Tourism Malaysia
Level 10, No. 2 Menara 1
Jalan P5/6, Presint 5
62200 Putrajaya, Kuala Lumpur
E-mail: mm2h@motour.gov.my
Tel: 03 8891 7434   Fax: 03 8891 7100

Department of Immigration, Sabah
Tingkat 6, Bangunan Wisma Dang Bandang
Jalan Tuanku Abdul Rahman
88550, Kota Kinabalu
Sabah, Malaysia
Tel: +6088–80700   Fax: +6088–240005

Department of Immigration, Sarawak
Tingkat 1 & 2, Bangunan Sultan Iskandar
Jalan Simpang Tiga
93550, Kuching, Sarawak, Malaysia
Tel: +6082–245661 / 240301 / 230317 / 230280 / 230314
Fax: +6088–240390/ 428606* Tourism Malaysia PWTC

Approval

Currently, from submission date, processing of documents and approval is supposed to take around 90 to 120 days. A backlog of applications, along with revised internal review program has stretched it longer. Five months is a more likely timetable.

Fees

A payment of $30 per year is charged for the issuance of a Social Visit Pass under the MM2H program. The visa fee is charged according to the existing rate applicable to each country. The fee for a ten-year visa, therefore, is $300; however, if the applicant's passport is valid for less than ten years, the visa will be valid only until the passport expiry date and the fee will be lower. Other visa charges may apply for certain nationalities but should not amount to more than $200 per person.

Visa Renewal Requirements

The applicant must be present in-person at the Malaysian Department of Immigration and bring the following documents:

- Letter explaining why you wish to renew the visa
- Original and photocopy of passport (certified true copy of every page)
- Form IMM.55 (one copy per person)
- Form IMM.38 (one copy if applicable)
- Proof of current offshore income of $3,300 or more per month
- Evidence that your fixed deposit is still in place
- Original and copy of confirmation letter from the bank (if applicable)
- Original and copy of conditional approval letter
- Original and copy of health insurance
- Original medical report (RB2 Form, which is available at MM2H Immigration Unit)
- Payment of $30 per year for the visa

Application for an Extension with New Passport

The visa is issued only for the period of your passport's validity. If you did not get the full term of the visa in your passport, you need to return to the immigration office in-person when you have a new passport to get the remainder of the visa stamped in your passport. The following documents are required for an extension:

- Letter of intention by the principal/sponsor (your agent)
- Copy of original approval letter
- Form IM.12
- Form IMM.55
- The original and a copy of both old and new passports for applicant and principal

MM2H Eligibility and Requirements

The MM2H program is open to all countries that are recognized by Malaysia.

A. Upon Application
1. **For applicants under 50 years of age:**
   - Required to show proof of higher liquid assets a minimum of $156,000, and offshore income of $3,200 per month.
   - Must provide certified copies of the latest three months' bank or investment statements showing each month's credit balance of $156,000 or more.
2. **For applicants aged 50 and over:**
   - Provide proof of $113,000 in liquid assets and offshore income of $3,200 per month.
   - Must provide the latest three months' bank or investment statements showing each month's credit balance of $113,000 or more.
   - Required to show proof of receiving a pension of $3,200 per month from government-approved funds.

- New applicants who have purchased property worth at least $330,000 qualify to place a lower fixed deposit amount upon approval.

B. Upon Approval

1. **For applicants under 50 years of age:**
   - Open a fixed deposit account of $100,000. After a period of one year, participants can withdraw up to $50,000 for approved expenses relating to house purchase, education for children in Malaysia, and medical purposes.
   - Must maintain a minimum balance of $50,000 from second year onwards and throughout stay in Malaysia under this program.

     Approved participants who own property in Malaysia bought for $330,000 or more may comply with the basic fixed deposit requirement of $50,000, on condition that the property has been fully paid for and ownership documents, such as grant and land title, have already been issued. This amount may not be withdrawn until the participant decides to terminate participation in the MM2H program.

2. **For applicants aged 50 and over:**
   - Open a fixed deposit account of $50,000. Note that applicants over 50 who can prove they receive a government pension in excess of $3,300 a month can request exemption from making the fixed deposit. After a period of one year, participants who fulfill the fixed deposit criterion can withdraw up to $16,000 for approved expenses relating to house purchase, education for children in Malaysia, and medical purposes.

- Must maintain a minimum balance of $34,000 from the second year onwards and throughout stay in Malaysia under this program.

  Approved participants who own property in Malaysia bought for $330,000 or more may comply with the basic fixed deposit requirement of $33,000, on condition that the property has been fully paid for and ownership documents, such as grant and land title, have already been issued. This amount may not be withdrawn until the participant decides to terminate participation in the MM2H program.

Medical Report

All applicants and their dependants are required to submit a medical report from any private hospital or registered clinic in Malaysia.

Medical Insurance

Approved participants and their dependants must possess valid medical insurance coverage that is applicable in Malaysia from any insurance company. But this next line is a real godsend and should be highlighted. So, I will:

"However, exemptions may be given for participants who face difficulty in obtaining a medical insurance due to their age or medical condition." Our experience is that an exemption is almost *always* given and that is a very good thing for a retiree.

Security Bond: Direct Applicant Only

Applicants applying directly are required to fulfill the security bond condition. The rate per person changes by nationality. At the time of writing, Canadians were paying about $300. Almost everyone uses an agent and, in fact, everyone should.

Personal Bond: Application Via Agent

Licensed companies are required to provide the personal bond for their clients who have been approved under the MM2H program.

Employment and Business Investment Rules

MM2H visa holders aged 50 years and over can work for up to twenty hours a week. This is applicable to visa holders who have specialized skills in certain approved sectors. We are advised that the decision about approval of part-time work is based on the approving committee's view on whether a Malaysian could do the job.

Visa holders are permitted to set up and invest in businesses in Malaysia. They will be subject to the same regulations as other foreign investors but will not be permitted to become actively involved in the day-to-day running of the business. If they wish to do this, they must switch their visa to a work permit.

Dependants

Applicants are allowed to bring along their dependants (children and stepchildren under 21 years of age, disabled children, and parents) under their MM2H visa. Older dependent children will have to get a separate visa. Dependants attending school in Malaysia are also required to apply for a student pass, which allows them to continue their education in schools or institutions of higher learning recognized by the government.

House Purchase

Each participant is allowed to buy an unlimited number of residences above the minimum applicable price set for foreigner purchasers in the state where the property is located. In most cases the minimum price is $330,000, although some states, like Penang, have higher minimums for MM2H visa holders. All purchases must be approved by the state authorities. Certain types of property cannot be purchased by foreigners, such as those on Malay Reserve Land.

Taxes
Successful applicants are subject to Malaysian taxes on income sourced from Malaysia, but income from overseas is not taxable.

Security Vetting
Approvals are given subject to security vetting clearance conducted by the Royal Malaysia Police. Applicants will also have to show a police clearance certificate (letter of good conduct) from their home country to prove they do not have a criminal record.

Restrictions
Successful applicants are not permitted to participate in activities that can be considered as sensitive by the local people, such as political or missionary activities.

Contacts
Malaysia My Second Home Centre
Ministry of Tourism Malaysia
Putra World Trade Centre
Level 34, Menara Dato' Onn
45 Jalan Tun Ismail
50695 Kuala Lumpur
E-mail: mm2h@motour.gov.my
Tel: +603 2693 7111

Immigration Department of Malaysia
(Kementerian Hal Ehwal Dalam Negeri)
Tingkat 1-7, (Podium) Blok 2G4, Precint 2,
Pusat Pentadbiran Kerajaan Persekutuan,
62550 Putrajaya, Wilayah Persekutuan
Tel: +603-88801000 Fax: +603-8881200
www.imi.gov.my

VIETNAM VISA

In black-and-white terms, a retiree who plans to live in Vietnam does not confront a visa problem—and that in itself is a problem. Vietnam does not issue retirement visas. The government issues tourist visas and long-term stay visas. But these long-term stay visas are issued only to diplomats and officials or for business and employment.

Tourist visas are available for a one-month stay and can be single entry or multiple entry.

What retirees to Vietnam normally do is extend these tourist visas. The initial visa is for thirty days. Then this visa is extended for an additional three months. This process, although not officially recognized, is then repeated every three months.

However, long-term foreign visitors are constantly concerned that one day their renewal request will be refused. This would then require them to leave the country and reapply for a fresh tourist visa.

In Canada, a tourist visa to Vietnam can be obtained online through the Vietnamese government embassy in Ottawa. The application form can be downloaded from www. VietnamVisa.ca. Simply complete the application form and send it online to the embassy's agent with a copy of your passport page, a regular passport photo, and your address. A summary of your application will be provided by email and, upon approval, your visa will arrive by mail or courier in four to seven days.

A business visa requires the sponsorship of a Vietnamese employer or business partner. This visa allows for multiple entries and a stay of up to one year. If you do not have a business partner, employer, or other sponsor who can provide you with an entry clearance, you can also apply for a business visa for a stay of up to ninety days.

Immigration agents in Vietnam can be used for this, and it does make the process much easier although more expensive. Extensions can be obtained via an agent within Vietnam.

CAMBODIA VISA

The Cambodian visa system is a simple one and there is little to add from our coverage in chapter 7. You can get a "visa on arrival" but the line-ups can be seriously daunting. Easier to use the embassy's visa service at www.cambodia.visacenter.ca.

You can do an e-visa online for a tourist visa. Business visas require a direct application with a sponsor letter. Extensions of the one-month term are available, but only at the Visa Centre at Phnom Penh airport and only for one additional month at a time, maximum ninety days. Business visas can be extended up to twelve months.

chapter 11

A Brief Guide
to Buying Property

Déjà vu? Does it feel like we've been here before? No worries. We have. In fact, we discussed property in each country chapter. But the requirements in Bali and Cambodia are more complex than the other destinations, so we've included more detail here. Seriously, don't feel bad about skipping this chapter if you have something better to do. Like checking out ads at Canadian Tire for a new snow blower.

BALI PROPERTY

It is illegal for foreigners to own freehold property—land, houses, villas, or apartments—in Bali. This restriction is written into the constitution. However, foreigners can legally buy leasehold property. The leases can be for at least twenty-five years plus a 30-year extension.

Some foreigners still insist on freehold ownership. We see this as presenting potentially serious problems. Nevertheless, it is quite common practice.

Foreign buyers can engineer freehold ownership in one of two ways:

1. **Use an Indonesian nominee**

   The nominee will sign the following four documents:
   - Loan agreement: this acknowledges that the foreigner has lent to the nominee the purchase price of the land
   - Right of use agreement: this allows the foreigner to use the land
   - Statement letter: this acknowledges the foreigner's loan and intention to own the land
   - Power of attorney: this irrevocably gives the foreigner the complete authority to sell, mortgage, lease, or otherwise deal in the land

2. **Use a company: a PMA**

   The most significant change in Indonesian investment law came in 1997 when the government introduced the Penanaman Modal Asing (PMA), or foreign investment company. This allows foreign investors to set up a company in Indonesia, without having to have Indonesian partners.

   The PMA can be 100 per cent owned by the foreign investor. PMA companies are allowed to own the title of the property for a period of twenty-five years. Then they must apply for their company status to be renewed by the government.

   To set up a PMA, you will be required to do the following:
   - Submit a detailed business plan

- Operate in a business environment that adds value to Indonesia in terms of foreign skills, employment, and environmental benefit
- Make an appropriate cash deposit in an Indonesian-based bank; the amount varies and is calculated on the capital employed in the business
- Show that there is property investment as an asset of the company

The process takes approximately three to four months, and once it is completed, the company can apply for work permits for the foreign directors—three permits in the first year of operation. The cost of setting up the PMA is between $2,600 and $3,600.

Fees

The following are required to be paid:

- Notary (see below): 1 per cent of the value of the transaction
- Vendor tax and purchaser tax: both the vendor and purchaser pay 5 per cent tax on the value of land and property sales
- Mortgage certificate: 1 per cent of value of mortgage

Get Expert Legal Advice

Remember, any effort to circumvent the law is a path fraught with potential heartache for the foreign purchaser.

To conclude a freehold property purchase with a local nominee, a notary is generally used. The notary creates the multi-party, multi-document legal construct that puts the freehold title in the hands of an Indonesian nominee.

By the way, a notary in Indonesia is a local legal expert registered as such by the Indonesian government.

The Indonesian nominee's name is on the property title and it is he or she who freeholds the parcel, not the foreign purchaser fronting the money for the land.

The notary will also usually create an irrevocable power of attorney in which the nominee owner surrenders all rights to use, sell, and lease the subject property to the foreign purchaser.

But is this legally enforceable? A foreigner may have to test this arrangement in court if in future he or she wishes to sell or transfer ownership/title to another party. This transfer will be heavily dependent on the good grace and continued docility of the Indonesian nominee who will need to attend the notary and sign over the deed to the new owner or their nominee.

There is one legal view that such contracts are from the very beginning *void ab initio* and therefore unenforceable in Indonesia. This is partly because the contract refers to a non-existent transfer of money between the parties during the so-called purchase transaction.

In early April 2015, the newly elected Indonesian government in Jakarta announced a review of all foreign-owned properties and related documents, especially targeting the freehold "nominee" system. Potentially, property bought using a "nominee" on the title will either legally be owned by the nominee or revert to the state. This is what we feared. Over time, there will be workarounds (this is Asia, after all); however, thousands of freehold property owners are not sleeping very well these days.

Good legal advice is essential if you wish to buy freehold property.

CAMBODIAN PROPERTY

Foreigners can own property in Cambodian buildings above the ground floor. This works well for apartments or even older buildings with several levels, like the top floor of a shop house.

The intention of the law is that foreigners cannot own land or houses, just above-ground-floor apartments.

A number of real estate agents and lawyers talk about mechanisms that allow foreigners to fully control the purchase, sale, and use of real property. They claim there are five options for buying real property (other than above-ground-floor apartments), which are as follows:

1. **Forming a company with a Cambodian citizen**
   Form a limited company in partnership with a Cambodian citizen. Any real property purchased for investment is then registered in the name of the company. The company must have a minimum 51 per cent Cambodian shareholding. However, careful allocation of shares and careful drafting of the rights attached to share certificates can ensure the foreigner's full control of the company and its assets. Additional mortgage, security, and power of attorney documents can also be created to accompany ownership documentation.

   Under this option, the foreigner is expected to pay 100 per cent of the purchase cost of real property plus any construction costs. If the real property is later sold, 100 per cent of the sale price goes directly to the foreigner. This includes any profit accrued as a result of the property increasing in value. This issue should be detailed carefully in any company and/or sales documentation.

2. **Purchase plus long-term rental**
   This method allows foreign nationals to purchase real property and register the title deed in the name of a Cambodian citizen. The foreigner and the Cambodian

then enter into a long-term rental agreement by which the Cambodian citizen leases the property back to the foreigner. Lease periods can last up to ninety-nine years.

The problem many foreigners have with this option is the concept of renting back property that has already been purchased.

However, correct drafting of the terms of the property holding and lease arrangements make this a reasonably secure method of controlling real property in Cambodia. Under this method, the foreigner may sell the property at any time and keep 100 per cent of the revenue from the sale. The Cambodian citizen is not permitted to disagree with or obstruct the sale. The foreigner retains the original copy of the new title deed as a security precaution: sale of real property is impossible without the original copy of the title deed.

Though the foreigner can sell the property at any time, the Cambodian citizen's signature or thumbprint is generally required before any sale can take place. A good working relationship between both parties is therefore very important.

3. **Registering real property with a Cambodian citizen**
    This method is very similar to option two, but requires complete trust in the Cambodian citizen.

    Foreign nationals have rights, under the kingdom's statutes, to choose a Cambodian in whose name their title deed is registered. That is, a foreign national can purchase property and register the purchased property in the name of the Cambodian citizen.

    Once the title deed is transferred to the Cambodian citizen, the foreigner retains possession of the new title deed. This is a security precaution that protects the

foreigner's interests by preventing the Cambodian citizen
from selling the land or property: sales are impossible
without the title deed. Transferring the Cambodian's
rights to the foreigner via a mortgage or lease agreement provides additional security for the foreigner's
investment.

Copies of the title deed and any mortgage or lease
agreements must be registered with the Department of
Provincial Land Management, Urban Planning and Construction, as well as the appropriate district and central
government departments that handle land registry. Most
importantly, a copy of the land title and any mortgage or
lease agreements must be lodged with the Cadastral Land
Registry Office.

The Cambodian citizen in whose name the title is
registered does not need to be resident in Cambodia. For
example, the title can be registered with a Cambodian
citizen living in Canada. The Cambodian citizen must be
able to prove Cambodian nationality.

4. Marriage to a Cambodian national

Foreign buyers who are married to a Cambodian national
can register real property using the name of their wife or
husband on the title deed. It is also possible for a foreign
national married to a Cambodian citizen and resident
in the country for a long period to apply for Cambodian
citizenship. In the event of citizenship being granted,
Cambodian law holds that land can be registered in the
names of both parties. Neither partner can subsequently
sell the land or property without mutual agreement.

In the event of divorce or separation, division of the
land or property is dependent on the conditions under
which divorce or separation takes place and the decision

of any court ruling or arbitration relating to the divorce. It is often a source of conflict between the divorcees.

5. **Acquisition of honorary Cambodian citizenship**
A foreigner may be granted honorary Cambodian citizenship if he or she donates a significant sum of money to the Royal Government of Cambodia for the purposes of benefiting the people of Cambodia. Foreigners who have made a special impact or rendered exceptional help to the kingdom may also be granted this honour in recognition of their expertise or altruism.

One consequence of being granted honorary citizenship is that it becomes possible for a foreign national to acquire a 100 per cent right of ownership over real property purchased within the kingdom. This arrangement is recognized by the Ministry of Land Management, Urban Planning and Construction for the Kingdom of Cambodia, and by the Royal Government.

Honorary citizenship is recognized by the Royal Government of Cambodia as a legitimate means of purchasing real property within the kingdom but it does not affect the foreigner's original nationality or citizenship in any way.

See? That wasn't really so bad. Okay, maybe it was. But all you need to really remember about property in Southeast Asia is this: explore the country first, meet with expats, engage with expat associations, ask questions, and if you want to buy, get professional, accredited help. Very often it isn't the law as written but the application of the law that matters.

What We've Learned

Retirement is a gift; it should be seen as a great opportunity. An early retirement is an even bigger gift, and if you are fortunate enough to sit in the bath a while longer to contemplate that opportunity, good for you. A new life, a productive, exciting life is around the corner.

Life is big. It can offer all kinds of adventures. But life is short too. You need to grab on to the good things—the ones that will make you happy and fulfilled—while you can.

It is often fear of the unknown or unfamiliar or fear of change that prevents us from leading a more interesting life. That is especially true as we get older, and the realities of our finances, our health, our cherished hopes and dreams start bubbling to the top of our agendas. Are we prepared?

There are nearly 10 million Canadians aged 44 to 64: the baby boomers. Many books have been written about them, many theories put forward about their impact on our culture, economy, and now even how their kids, the Gen Xers, will take their place.

Many Canadians of this BB cohort are well prepared for their impending retirement. They got married, had kids, saved, invested, bought and paid for property, inherited wealth, and accumulated enough to be secure and comfortable. They have achieved all they had hoped for. They are set.

As we said at the outset, this book is not for them.

A great number of baby boomers, millions of them, may well be facing an uncertain future. They may have not saved enough to live those additional years good health has granted them. The financial crisis of 2008–2009 may have interrupted a slow and steady accumulation of wealth in their RRSPs or savings accounts. The kids were more expensive than they thought and aren't exactly leaving home in quite the rush that we used to in the 60s or 70s.

There are no guaranteed company pensions anymore, unless you were smart enough to jump out of the private sector and into the public one, no matter that it didn't seem very sexy at the time. Governments can't help you—it is all they can do to keep the old promises made to keep CPP intact, and even that isn't guaranteed more than a few years down the road anymore. Our health care system, of which we are so rightly proud, is stretched. Medical appointment times have gone from days to weeks to months. And what happens when a system geared to critical care has to shift to care for millions, many millions, of aging Canadians?

When the idea of this book—about creating a new and less expensive life in Southeast Asia—was discussed with our Australian partners, we spent hours debating the practical issues. Once we understood why it would work, it came down to how. It became obvious to us that our own voices would not be enough. We needed to talk to people in every country we cover who had done it, who sought another kind of life than the one that had them aging in place at home. For many people, the decision was purely economic; for others it was to find the thrill again; for some it was both. We think these real-life, real-time stories show it can be done and how it can be a wonderful and life-changing experience.

We hope our collective efforts have inspired some of you to take control of the rest of your lives. We hope the interviews we've shared show the why and the how and that at least a few of the stories go straight to your heart and to your head. It can work for you too.

Before you take the leap, there are a bucket of questions—in addition to the ones we've already posed—you need to address.

How happy are you really? Do you think a change in lifestyle would enhance and enrich your existence? What should be on your consideration checklist? What sort of financial advantages or disadvantages are there for you in a shift to another country? What are the best strategies for you to follow to realize that dream retirement, or at least to test the waters? Should you leave Canada full time or just take a few months' sabbatical to refresh and recharge? And, for older Canadians, there will come a time when you will need care. What would that be like—being a burden to your kids, paying for an expensive private facility, living in a public institution, or putting yourself in the hands of a caregiver in a faraway place?

The many people we met moved for a variety of reasons and chose their new country on just as wide a range of criteria. For some it was a happy accident triggered by an inspirational visit. For others it was a thorough, analytical process of investigation and elimination based on key needs and wants.

Kendall and her family's new life in Malaysia was launched by a heartfelt conversation with friends and more than a few bottles of red wine. Not old enough to retire, they wanted a new challenge and they found it.

Bob and Marion were much more thorough. Bob set down the criteria for them to isolate the perfect country that met all their retirement needs, now and in the future. He looked at health care, taxation, crime, cost of living, and cultural fit in great detail. They too chose Malaysia, specifically Penang, and they have never regretted it.

With few exceptions, most of the people we met were absolutely convinced that their decision to move to another country, for whatever their personal reasons, was the right one.

That said, you *can* go home again. Many of those now living the dream in Phuket or Penang for a few months or a few years may well return to Canada. Some dreams fade over time and the pull of our wonderful country is always strong. One thing to remember, the people we met all took the chance and will never die wondering, "What if?" is a question they will never have to ask themselves as they look into the mirror.

THE FRAMEWORK

1. The starting point for any strategy is to know yourself. Having a clear view of the sort of life you want to live. Do you dream of the beach, the countryside, the mountains, or the city? Does the idea of a foreign country appeal to you, and what sort of culture and environment attracts you? Does a foreign language dissuade you or inspire you? Can you craft a set of criteria that acts as your "must have" list? Is it an economic change you seek or a new and more inspiring lifestyle?

2. You need to understand the health and medical issues you will confront. Balance what the different countries offer with your current needs and project what requirements you could have in the future. If you have heart disease or diabetes today, a robust medical capability is an absolute country criterion you will need.

3. You need to understand the visa requirements of the countries you are considering. We talk in this book at length about these issues but keep in mind that all governments, including ours, do change their policies. You will want to pick the one that is the most stable, the most consistent, and the most expat-friendly.

4. You need to understand the tax policies of the countries you are considering. But most importantly, you must understand the policies of our own country. Canada has tax treaties with many, but not all, countries; some favour the expat and some less so. Our country also has strict rules about how many days you can spend out of the country and still maintain your residency and all your benefits. And if you're considering a permanent move you should be fully aware of the "ties that bind." Owning a home, having a driver's licence, a bank account, a credit card, a car are all major or minor threads that our government uses to determine if you have really left the country or are just intending to avoid taxes and return when it is convenient.

5. It is important to visualize where and how you would like to live as you grow older. There are several choices to consider—entering old-age accommodation in a facility in Canada or staying at home in Southeast Asia with a full-time, affordable caregiver. Full-time home care costs a fortune in Canada—it does not in Asia.

6. Knowing yourself also means that you know your financial position and how much your lifestyle options will cost at home or away. Our investigations clearly indicate a minimum 50 per cent reduction in the cost of living in Southeast Asia, more in some countries. And even a part-time move (say, the six months Canada allows you to live overseas in a year) can save you considerable money if you sell or rent your home in Canada.

7. Self-analysis of your financials is crucial. If you have nothing in your RRSP and no pension from your company, but you own your house outright, selling it will not fund your retirement at home unless it is a mansion. But even a modest house sale of $600,000 to $800,000 could fund you in Southeast Asia for a very long time. Think of Bob and Marion in Penang and their thirtieth-floor penthouse for $2,100 a month. Then think about something only a little more modest for $1,000 less; and then, if you drop a bedroom and bathroom or take a lower floor, take another few hundred off that. The idea is to stretch what you have but live in real comfort, and you can do that all over Southeast Asia.

8. You have heard it throughout the book: *rent before buying*. Without attempting to give an economics lesson here, the Asian property investor is putting pots of money into property as that culture sees property as the only real safe haven. They don't trust banks, they don't trust the stock market, but they do trust property. They invest in condos and villas for long-haul appreciation but the truth is they really need a place to put their money. Renters are just placeholders for them, and expat renters are the best of all. If you must buy, make sure you clearly understand the country's rules and how they

might change. Please, get expert legal assistance and trust nobody else.

THE FINALE ... OR THE BEGINNING

I have often cruised the business section of Indigo in Toronto or Kinokuniya Books in Singapore or Page One in Hong Kong and wondered what really gave an author the credibility to wax on about his subject.

Some of you who have gotten this far may be asking the same question about us.

Here is your answer. We did it.

After five years in Singapore and three in China, we realized our nomadic life abroad had reached a point where we had to make a change. While we had money, a lot by some standards, we had taken a beating in the financial crisis and, although we clawed back our losses, we lost years of growth that we won't get back. Our consultancy business had boomed for the first few years but global budget cuts had hurt us badly, and it wasn't ever going to be as robust as it was. In a moment of frustration over a visa issue with the Singapore authorities, we had thrown in our crayons and bought a not inexpensive Yorkville condo pre-construction that was going to suck up our reserves and still require a mortgage or line of credit when it was finished. We needed to make more money and to slow the burn rate of the money we had.

And, after five good-to-great years, we were tiring of Singapore. It had become a terribly expensive place to live, by some measures the most expensive city in the world. The politics of the city-state were becoming more and more unfriendly to expats, and it was increasingly run more like the one-party family business it really is than the democracy it pretends to be.

Don't get me wrong—it is an economic miracle and one of the most fantastic cities in the world. We just didn't want to live there anymore feeling as we did and, even if we wanted to, we could not afford the lifestyle we had been accustomed to.

Then our Australian friends, Steve Wyatt and Colleen Ryan, whom we had met while living in China, told us about a book they were writing for Aussies, a book about retiring in Southeast Asia. We had a sleepless night and called them back in the morning with an idea. We could write a second book for Canadians as the demographics of baby boomers, the pension systems, and the health care systems were all going to be similarly challenged in Canada. They graciously let us in to their process as full partners for this and future books. We hit the ground running.

Ellen and I had been to all the places covered in this book but one. Some places we had considered moving to in the past but there was always something that came up: bad weather, bad politics, bad services, lack of community—something that prevented us from making the leap.

As for that one destination we missed? I suggested to Ellen that in all our years in Asia we had never been to Penang and that, to be true to the book, we had to go and see it, talk to people, and form an opinion. It wasn't crucial, since Steve and Colleen had been there, but we felt we needed a Canadian perspective in every market, and so we went.

Our first weekend on Penang Island was one part revelation and one part inspiration. We stayed at the gorgeous Seven Terraces hotel, ate at Kebaya and ChinaHouse, drove past the gorgeous condos off Gurney Drive and north up to Tanjung Bungah. With our hired car and driver, we went further north to Batu Ferringhi's beaches and all the way around the island past the durian fruit stands and through the nature reserve.

Returning home to Singapore, we felt we could do this. I hired a real estate agent and an immigration agent to process our MM2H visa application; in the process, we realized Penang was going to be our next home.

A few weeks later we went back. With our outstanding agent Charlene Sim from Pen Properties, we toured a half-dozen condos, seeing two or three or four suites in each building. This time we stayed in the Heritage Wing of the venerable Eastern & Oriental Hotel, a wonderful old British pile that pre-dated Raffles Singapore by ten years. We had dinner at The Mansion, checked out the malls and grocery stores, and by the end of the weekend decided to make an offer to rent a condo at 8 Gurney Drive.

We chose 8 Gurney primarily for its location: a walk to the two big malls down the waterfront and a walk to the shops and restaurants of old Georgetown in the other direction. The condo is enormous—5,800 square feet with five bedrooms and bathrooms, a giant kitchen, and a 360-degree balcony as each unit is one full floor. There is an open Chinese wet kitchen off the main kitchen where I put my BBQ, and the entire place has ten ceiling fans—four in the living room alone! We have a view over the water on one side, the old town on another, and the mountains on another. There are fantastic sunrises over the sea and the far shore of the mainland and sunsets over the mountains behind us. The pool facing the water is huge, as is the gym, and we got four times the space for 50 per cent of what we paid in Singapore. All seemed good and then …

We got off to a rough start. The condo was too big, our shipped goods were in Singapore storage waiting for news of our visas, we missed our friends in Singapore, and we knew not one soul in Penang. The first two weeks were kind of bleak. Then, in week three we decided to just go ahead, land our goods, and pay whatever duties and taxes the Malaysian authorities applied even though we had not received our visa yet. To our surprise, they applied none. We went to dinner to celebrate at a cozy spot called That Little Wine Bar, where we found they had a wine-tasting meet-and-greet every Thursday. Now we go every week and all the patrons have become our friends. Ellen made another friend on the web—a Canadian of all people—who has been simply brilliant at showing us the ropes around town. And then we took the opportunity to contact Bob and Marion, whom you know so well from the Malaysian chapter. Last week we had all our pals from the wine bar, and Bob and Marion, to our house for our first big dinner party for ten.

It is early days yet. But we have found our footing, and things are looking great. The friendliness of the local people is outstanding. As Bob says, the concentrated and like-minded expat population here makes an island of 700,000 feel more like a friendly village. Penang's reputation for wonderful food is richly deserved as we have had simply outstanding meals all over town for a fraction of what we would pay in Singapore or at home in Canada. The local wet market is wonderful, clean, and bright with good prices and no gouging of expats—one price for all with no haggling. I found Mr. Teoh, who flies in fresh salmon from British Columbia every Friday, and we get our New Zealand beef and lamb from Fresh Yields, a short drive away. Cellphone contracts are dirt cheap with great service; the Astro cable TV has even more selection than Singapore. HSBC bank has been helpful to the point of coming to our hotel on a Saturday to open up our bank accounts.

Try suggesting that to RBC or BMO.

We applied for the MM2H visa and got our approval five months later; not the sixty to ninety days they promise. Seems there is a backlog of applications. As I said at the outset, you will not be alone here. We have six months to activate the visa and, at this writing, we can think of no reason not to.

We may return to Toronto in the long term, we may not. It has crossed our minds that a slightly less extravagant place here in Penang would allow us to keep a foot in both camps. Time will tell, as we have more than a year to make that decision. We have taken the first step.

The fact remains, in the coming decades there are going to be millions of Canadian retirees facing decisions like we had to make. The demographics of Western societies all point to a virtual tsunami of aging populations. Health services will be stretched and governments may not be able to maintain funding services as costs rise. Pensions could be pared back as a shrinking work force can't support a swelling cohort of retirees. Housing and services for older people won't be able to keep up with demand.

The retirement possibilities at home that we all are facing are creating circumstances where it is going to be harder and harder for most of us to thrive, let alone all of us survive.

In this book we have mapped out an alternative: fifteen places in Southeast Asia where you can build a new life—a life that costs less but also inspires; an elixir of change, adventure, and a bold new beginning.

Come and see for yourself.

Or, for more and updated information, go to our website: www.planet-boomer.com.

Acknowledgements

We are very grateful to the many dozens of fascinating people who shared part of their lives with us, patiently answered our detailed questions, and put up with our endless follow-ups. They allowed us to bring you their stories of what it is really like to live and retire in Southeast Asia.

Their generosity with their own time, and their kindness in introducing us to other people in their expat circle, was invaluable. Most were comfortable with the use of their real names. Others, for reasons of privacy, preferred to use pseudonyms. To be consistent, the names of all our interviewees have been changed.

Thanks also to Sarah Barlow, Jonathan Schmidt, Zoja Popovic, and Kyle Gell of Barlow Books for their patience and perseverance. Especially to Jonathan Schmidt who, on any given day around revision 10, wanted to throttle me as much as I wanted to beat on him. Thank you.

Ellen and I want to particularly thank Stephen Wyatt and Colleen Ryan, our Australian friends and partners, who came up with the idea for this book and ploughed the field for us in so many ways. We have had an extraordinary time together: many laughs, much white wine and great food. In my life I have attended thousands of meetings. Any time spent with Steve and Col beats any other meeting I've ever had by a country mile.

And, to my partner and wife, Ellen, who kept the fire burning all these months to get the writing done, pushing the idea ever forward while creating our website and doing about 500 other things at the same time—thank you.

And finally, to you the reader: We took this on as a mission, in our strong belief that this book, these stories, can truly help many Canadians live a better, fuller life in Southeast Asia while stretching their resources further than they ever thought possible at home. We hope it helps.

For more information on the countries, the people, and their stories, visit our website: www.planet-boomer.com.

About the Authors

After a combined sixty years in marketing communications, Jim Herrler and Ellen Ma now live in Penang. They like to think they are living this book as it was the book's research that convinced them to pack up after five years in Singapore and move to yet another country, their fourth Asian destination in nine years (well, twice in Singapore if you really want to count).

Jim's career in Canadian advertising spanned thirty-five years from Vickers & Benson to MacLaren McCann, to JWT and then to DDB, where he ended his advertising agency life as president of the company's Toronto operations. His years in the wilderness since then were anything but dull. He worked for a Saudi prince, counselled clients in Shanghai, and, in partnership with Ellen, created an innovation consulting company based in Singapore that achieved remarkable success.

Ellen Ma came to Canada from Taiwan as an eight-year-old. Her career began in advertising with JWT, then at DMB&B with a jump to the client side with IBM. That path took her to New York and Japan before she settled back in Canada as VP Marketing for Shoppers Drug Mart. A move to Singapore with Cisco Systems followed and then a shift in focus to innovation consulting with ?Whatif! based in Shanghai. Her own innovation consulting company, Co-Innovate, followed, and she has now run innovation projects and taught innovation techniques to multiple clients in twenty-six countries around the world.

Both Jim and Ellen believe their experiences abroad have enriched their lives, but they remain true Canadians at heart: when finding a turkey in China on Canadian Thanksgiving proved impossible, they tied the parts of two big chickens together and made ... well, not sure what that was but they tried.

Planet Boomer

For more information
on the countries, the people,
and their stories, visit

www.planet-boomer.com